TOYOTOMI HIDEYOSHI

LEADERSHIP ▪ STRATEGY ▪ CONFLICT

STEPHEN TURNBULL

First published in Great Britain in 2010 by Osprey Publishing,
Midland House, West Way, Botley, Oxford OX2 0PH, UK
44-02 23rd St, Suite 219, Long Island City, NY 11101, USA

E-mail: info@ospreypublishing.com

A CIP catalogue record for this book is available from the British Library.

ISBN: 978 1 84603 960 7
E-book ISBN: 978 1 84603 961 4

Editorial by Ilios Publishing Ltd, Oxford, UK (www.iliospublishing.com)
Page layout by Myriam Bell Design, France
Index by Auriol Griffith-Jones
Typeset in Stone Serif and Officina Sans
Maps by The Mapping Specialists Ltd.
Originated by PDQ Media, Bungay, UK
Printed in China through Worldprint Ltd

10 11 12 13 14   10 9 8 7 6 5 4 3 2 1

Dedication

For my grandson Laurence Alexander Turnbull, born 4 December 2009.

Artist's note

Readers may care to note that the original paintings from which the
colour plates in this book were prepared are available for private sale.
The Publishers retain all reproduction copyright whatsoever.
All enquiries should be addressed to:

Giuseppe Rava, Via Borgotto 17, Faenz, 48018, Italy

The Publishers regret that they can enter into no correspondence upon
this matter.

Editor's note

All pictures are from the author's collection.

Title page caption

This fine statue of Hideyoshi as a general has only recently been restored
to public view after a long period of storage. It is now stands within the
grounds of Osaka Castle, the great edifice created by Hideyoshi on the
site of the former fortress/cathedral of Ishiyama Honganji.

FOR A CATALOGUE OF ALL BOOKS PUBLISHED BY OSPREY
MILITARY AND AVIATION PLEASE CONTACT:

Osprey Direct, c/o Random House Distribution Center,
400 Hahn Road, Westminster, MD 21157
Email: uscustomerservice@ospreypublishing.com

Osprey Direct, The Book Service Ltd, Distribution Centre,
Colchester Road, Frating Green, Colchester, Essex, CO7 7DW
E-mail: customerservice@ospreypublishing.com

www.ospreypublishing.com

The Woodland Trust
Osprey Publishing are supporting the Woodland Trust, the UK's
leading woodland conservation charity, by funding the
dedication of trees.

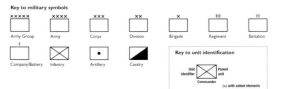

CONTENTS

INTRODUCTION

In this scroll painting in the Hosei Niko Exhibition Hall, we see Hideyoshi as a general in full armour. This is the perfect image of the great statesman in the crucial military role that achieved the unification of Japan. On the shoulder plates of his suit of armour appear the *mon* (badge) of paulownia that was flown from the flags of his army.

Toyotomi Hideyoshi (1536–98), whose grand campaigns and rise to power have led to him being compared to Napoleon Bonaparte, was responsible for bringing Japan out of the division of the Sengoku Jidai (The Age of Warring States) and into the unity of an age of elegance, economic growth and political consolidation. Yet none of this could have been achieved without the military campaigns that had both preceded and brought about the political solution. Furthermore, even though Hideyoshi's immense skills in negotiation with cautious allies and his revolutionary generosity to defeated enemies were vital factors in achieving his ambitious goals, he could not have treated his enemies in such a way if he had not first defeated them, nor won debates with rivals if he had not had the military authority ultimately to overawe them.

Hideyoshi's reunification of Japan was a colossal military undertaking carried out successfully by the son of a farmer who had fought as a foot soldier; and for Hideyoshi his earliest military challenges were to be provided by the question of his own survival. This involved the crucial choice as to which of several masters he might follow, and having chosen one and provided loyal service until that lord's death there began the second question of how he could benefit from that unexpected development and achieve for himself the goal to which his late master had been working. From that moment on the experience of command that he had gained in the service of another provided the foundations for superb generalship in his own right, first at a tactical and then at a strategic level, where all the military and political resources he

possessed came together to unite Japan under his sword. On his death in 1598 this was the legacy he passed on to his infant son Hideyori, whose minority was sadly to be exploited by rivals, one of whom was to seize what Hideyoshi believed he had secured for his own descendants. Yet in the regime that followed, a dynasty that was to last for 250 years, all the political institutions that sustained it could be traced back to innovations that had taken advantage of the situation of peace and unity achieved through the military campaigns of Toyotomi Hideyoshi, Japan's greatest commander.

THE EARLY YEARS

The world into which Toyotomi Hideyoshi was born in 1536 was a realm characterized by rivalry and strife, where competing daimyo (the Japanese samurai lords) challenged each other for local and eventually national supremacy. Yet this time of war was far from being simply an age of chaos. That era had largely passed into history three decades earlier, when the first petty daimyo to have emerged from the convulsions of the mid-15th century had either disappeared into well-deserved oblivion or succeeded in establishing mini-kingdoms large and secure enough to provide an ordered, if somewhat hazardous, life for those fortunate enough to live under their benevolent rule.

The bestowal upon their followers of paternalistic leadership and material reward, and the receipt in return of loyalty and service on the battlefield and in the rice field was the mutually beneficial arrangement that had characterized local politics in Japan since 1467, the year that saw the beginning of the terrible Onin War. Up until that time the central point of authority in Japan was located in the person of the shogun, the military dictator, a post created in 1192 within the Minamoto family following their triumph in the Gempei War. By 1467 the shogunate had long been in the hands of the Ashikaga family, who had seized power following a disastrous attempt during the fourteenth century to restore the power of the divine emperor of Japan, whose rule since 1192 had been largely ceremonial and religious. The Ashikaga had occasionally been forced to deal with rebels and disputes between landowners during the century through which they had ruled, but throughout all these convulsions the centre had held firm.

This scroll painting of Hideyoshi in formal court robes hangs in Karatsu castle. He is shown holding a war fan ornamented with red silk and pearls.

In 1467 everything was to change. A succession dispute within the shogun's own family set at odds a number of the most powerful samurai families of Japan. Much of the immediate fighting took place within the capital city of Kyoto itself, and, as wide areas of that fine imperial and shogunal city were destroyed, so too was the reputation and authority of the shogunate. The crucial losses among the shogun's powers included the absolute right to appoint deputies to govern and tax distant provinces, to raise troops and to go to war. This collapse of authority therefore ushered in a golden age of opportunity for any warrior willing to try his hand. These men were the first daimyo, and what a disparate bunch they were! Some belonged to quite ancient families that were well-established in their domains, whose ancestors had once pledged allegiance to the shogun and received in return a commission to rule locally in the shogun's name. Others were simply military opportunists, who seized power in their localities by murder and mayhem and went on to defend their little territories from the safety of mountaintop castles using armies of samurai. As the years went by certain territories grew larger at the expense of others. These fortunate realms were better governed and better led by men whose skills in warfare were their most important accomplishments, so that by the 1530s several considerable domains existed where one might have found a settled environment of agriculture, commerce and culture that mimicked the sophistication of the now largely impotent shogunate in all but scale.

For many of the future daimyo of Japan who were born around 1536 their road to greatness began with birth into comparative greatness and then, perhaps, service during boyhood as a page in one of the greater households. This process was put into operation on several occasions as a formal hostage system, but less cynical applications of it could result in alliances that would hold firm for decades and provided a form of training for a young warrior that was second to none.

Yet this was not a path that would be followed by Toyotomi Hideyoshi. His father, Yaemon, had indeed provided military service to their local hegemon, a comparatively successful daimyo called Oda Nobuhide, but it was not employment of the sort that would lead to his son serving tea in Nobuhide's castle, because Yaemon was only a local farmer. He put in occasional service in the Oda army, probably as no more than a foot soldier, yet Yaemon was no downtrodden peasant. He would not have been press-ganged into the army or even conscripted. He owned his own parcel of land and would probably have been motivated to go to war by a combination of reward and glory, although Yaemon was definitely not of the samurai class. The opportunity for such promotion may well have been his for the taking, because in those days bravery in warfare could lead to considerable personal advancement, but Yaemon was wounded during one campaign and thereafter permanently invalided out of Nobuhide's army. He returned to his fields and died in 1543, leaving an elder daughter and a seven-year-old son called Tokichiro, the boy who was to be the future Toyotomi Hideyoshi.

In later years Hideyoshi would tell anyone who cared to listen that when he had been conceived his mother had had a wonderful dream whereby the room was filled with sunlight. This had been a mark of his destiny, indicating that his virtue would shine over the seas and that his glory would radiate in all directions. Absent was any acknowledgement of his humble birth or the tragedy of his father's early death. In their place grew further legends of Hideyoshi as an infant prodigy who organized the children of the village in mock warfare, but in fact we know almost nothing of his childhood until he

This modern woodblock print shows Hideyoshi in armour in front of a background of a *maku* (field curtain) bearing his paulownia *mon*. He is wearing a helmet with the rear crest of a sunburst, an allusion to the manufactured story that when Hideyoshi was conceived a miraculous burst of sunlight filled the room as promise of his future greatness.

emerges as an ambitious adolescent warrior seeking service in about 1551 in the nearby province of Totomi. His chosen master was a certain Matsushita Yukitsuna, the minor retainer of the local daimyo Imagawa Yoshimoto (1519–60). This was such a surprising career move that it is very likely to be true, because the Imagawa were the sworn enemies of the Oda of Owari province, whom Hideyoshi's father had served; so what we are probably seeing is an ambitious young Hideyoshi seeking military glory with any daimyo who was willing to take him on. The venture did not succeed, because we know that by 1558 he had abandoned Matsushita and was back in Owari serving Oda Nobunaga (1534–82), the son and heir of Oda Nobuhide. With this move Hideyoshi's military career really began.

This modern statue of Hideyoshi as a boy stands near the shrine in Nakamura, now a suburb of Nagoya, built on the supposed site of Hideyoshi's birth. Like many great heroes, there are tales of Hideyoshi as an infant prodigy organizing the boys of his village in mock warfare.

THE MILITARY LIFE

Hideyoshi's decision to return to Owari province and serve the Oda family as his father had done before him was the beginning of a relationship with Oda Nobunaga that would last for 24 years. Oda Nobunaga is one of the pivotal figures in Japanese history. He was the second son of Oda Nobuhide, and spent the first years of his military career disposing of rivals within his own family and asserting personal control over the whole of the province. He also faced rivals from outside Owari, particularly from the Imagawa, and Hideyoshi's decision to abandon the Imagawa cause and rejoin the Oda in 1558 took place at a very important time in the destiny of both families.

Imagawa Yoshimoto, warlord and aesthete, ruled his provinces from a 'little Kyoto', where he enjoyed the pleasures of art and literature to a degree that was perhaps a little unwise for someone who was surrounded by enemies. Yet Yoshimoto's political ambitions were the equal of his aesthetic sensibilities, and he was able to back them up by the service of a large and loyal army. His position on the Tokaido road, the main communication route between eastern and western Japan along the Pacific coast, placed him in a situation where he, alone among the 'super-daimyo' who had emerged from the early Sengoku Period, could contemplate marching from his imitation Kyoto to the real thing, there to depose the shogun or (for this was Japan, a place where tradition matters) to force the current incumbent to bend to his will.

The first objective that Imagawa Yoshimoto had to overcome on his journey to the capital was the adjacent province of Owari, ruled by Oda Nobunaga. Imagawa Yoshimoto would never have known that a minor warrior in his service who would one day be called Hideyoshi had decided

Almost the whole of Hideyoshi's military career prior to 1582 was carried out in the service of Oda Nobunaga, to whom Hideyoshi showed constant loyalty at whatever level of command. Hideyoshi fought for Nobunaga at the famous battles of Anegawa and Nagashino. This *ema* (votive painting) depicting Nobunaga and his men hangs in the Okumura House in Inuyama.

to abandon him in 1558 for the Oda. If Yoshimoto had known this he would probably have laughed at the ignominious foot soldier's foolish decision, because Yoshimoto was planning to march through Owari with an army ten times the strength of the Odas' force. We do not know for certain if Hideyoshi took any active part in the series of battles that ensued, of which Imagawa Yoshimoto won every encounter except the last. In that fateful meeting, the battle of Okehazama in 1560, Oda Nobunaga deprived him of his head, and Yoshimoto's march on Kyoto came to an ignominious end.

The battle of Okehazama confirmed Oda Nobunaga's military skills, and among those skills was the ability to attract to his side men of talent and to appreciate such gifts regardless of a person's humble birth, so low-born Hideyoshi prospered in the service of the Oda. One of the most popular stories concerning Hideyoshi's early years with Nobunaga tells of his being employed as Nobunaga's sandal bearer, a post equivalent to being the daimyo's batman, and endearing himself to his master by warming the straw sandals inside his own shirt during winter time. It is an attractive image that combines the traditional samurai virtues of devotion and loyalty with a clever appreciation of how to win friends and influence people, but Hideyoshi's major contribution to Oda Nobunaga was in the military sphere, where he assisted his master at each successive level of promotion to which he was appointed.

With the destruction of Imagawa Yoshimoto and the virtual neutering of his heir, Oda Nobunaga was established as a considerable military leader in his own right, and after consolidating his own position within Owari he could begin to contemplate success in precisely the same ambitious field where Yoshimoto had failed. One day Nobunaga would take Kyoto and control the shogun; and he began by directing his efforts against the neighbouring province of Mino.

During Nobunaga's consolidation of Owari he had received support from Mino's daimyo Saito Dosan Toshimasa (1494–1556), a man who had personified the opportunistic environment of the early Sengoku Period by making the transition from oil merchant to daimyo in one giant leap. Nobunaga had wisely married Dosan's daughter, but with Dosan's death in 1556 Mino became enemy territory once again. His son Saito Yoshitatsu (1527–61) opposed Nobunaga until dying from the effects of leprosy in 1561, and the conflict was continued by Yoshitatsu's heir Saito Tatsuoki (1548–73). The war between Nobunaga and Tatsuoki was a long one in which Hideyoshi took an active part, although accounts vary of what he actually did in the series of campaigns that won Mino province for the Oda. One story has Hideyoshi's men climbing up the mountain of Inabayama, on the peak of which the final refuge of the Saito was situated, and then signalling to Hideyoshi below by waving the gourds they had carried up as water canteens attached to their spears. Hideyoshi subsequently used the image of a gourd as part of his heraldic display. Another story, eminently believable, has Hideyoshi placed in charge of building a fortress on the very edge of enemy territory at nearby Sunomata from where the attack could be launched. This is in perfect accordance with later views of Hideyoshi as a master of strategy and logistics, although the common embellishment of the Sunomata story has Hideyoshi completing the building of it overnight. The resulting 'fortress' was no more than a two-dimensional 'film set' of laths and paper that inevitably overawed the Saito by the speed of its construction.

One of the most telling legends concerning Hideyoshi's early service to Nobunaga involves him warming Nobunaga's sandals inside his own shirt, thus expressing a neat combination of traditional self-sacrificing samurai values and an appreciation of how to win favour from a superior. This scene is from *Ehon Toyotomi Kunkoki*, an illustrated life of Hideyoshi with woodblock illustrations by Kuniyoshi.

There is some confusion over the year when Nobunaga captured Inabayama, which he was to rename Gifu and make into his own capital. The most likely scenario is that Nobunaga captured Inabayama in 1564 and then lost it again to Tatsuoki in 1565, finally securing it in 1567. He was now lord of two provinces, and ready to begin his advance on Kyoto. This he undertook successfully in 1568, riding into the city triumphantly with a young man called Ashikaga Yoshiaki (1537–97). Yoshiaki was the brother of a former shogun who had been murdered, and a cousin of the present shogun appointed by the ringleader of the plot: Matsunaga Hisahide (1510–77). Yoshiaki had appealed to various daimyo to assist in his attempts to become shogun, and in 1568 he found one in the person of Oda Nobunaga, a man who had both the ambition and the resources to help him. The Matsunaga forces fled as Nobunaga approached Kyoto and soon afterwards Nobunaga's nominee was appointed to the post of shogun. Yoshiaki was to be the last of his line, and for the next five years he was to struggle vainly against the man who had put him into a position of power but was to prevent him exercising it. Throughout this time we may imagine Hideyoshi providing diligent, successful, loyal and humble service within the ranks of Nobunaga's army, giving a solid performance enlivened by moments of genius.

By 1570 Hideyoshi's military service becomes more reliably recorded, and he is confirmed that year as being a leader of 3,000 men within Nobunaga's army. This was during a campaign against one of Nobunaga's most serious enemies, the daimyo Asakura Yoshikage (1533–73). The Asakura ruled Echizen province to the north of the capital, and had not failed to demonstrate their lack of approval for the upstart Oda Nobunaga when he took Kyoto in 1568. In 1570 Nobunaga decided to assess the degree of support he could command from the daimyo surrounding him by summoning them to come and pay their respects to the new shogun. Asakura Yoshikage's refusal to attend provided Nobunaga with the excuse to attack him, so Nobunaga set off at the head of an allied army in the spring of 1570. Hideyoshi, now allowed to make immediate operational decisions himself, wrote one of his earliest surviving letters to a merchant in Sakai requesting supplies of gunpowder for the fort he had been ordered to defend.

Nobunaga's initial progress into Echizen was very successful. He captured a series of fortresses and was within striking distance of the Asakura capital of Ichijodani when worrying news was brought to him. Asai Nagamasa (1545–73), Nobunaga's brother-in-law, had entered into an alliance with the Asakura. Nagamasa's position in northern Omi province meant that he was able to cut off Nobunaga's means of retreat and even subject the Oda army to a two-pronged attack while they were isolated from more distant support. Nobunaga had no choice but to attempt a rapid withdrawal from Echizen before any such move could be set in motion. Fortunately, Kuchiki Mototsuna (1549–1632), lord of the castle of Kuchiki in Omi province, agreed to guide Nobunaga's army along the maze of narrow mountain paths that bypassed the main communication routes to the north-west of Lake Biwa and back to

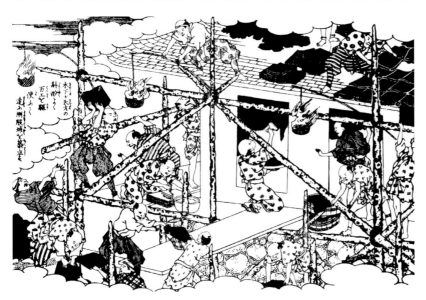

During the campaign against the Saito of Mino province, Hideyoshi was given the difficult task of establishing a defensive position at Sunomata from where an attack could be launched. Sunomata, however, was a strategic point overlooked by the enemy. Hideyoshi achieved his objective, and later legend embellished the story to have him erect a dummy fortress overnight that consisted of little more than laths and paper, thus overawing the Saito by the speed of its miraculous construction. This scene is from *Ehon Toyotomi Kunkoki*.

Kyoto through the district of Ohara, thus avoiding any move by the Asai. For this to succeed the Asakura army had to be held back. This dangerous role was accepted by two outstanding men who were then fighting with Nobunaga. The first was his ally the famous Tokugawa Ieyasu (1542–1616). The second was Toyotomi Hideyoshi. They appear to have worked very well together, coordinating their efforts and supporting each other when hard pressed.

When Nobunaga next marched against the Asai and Asakura both Ieyasu and Hideyoshi were again with him. As befitted their differing status with regard to Nobunaga, Tokugawa Ieyasu led an allied army while the subordinate Hideyoshi was given command of the troops that Nobunaga had raised from Omi province, whose loyalty to either the

This woodblock print shows Hideyoshi with his 'thousand gourd' battle standard. The use of the gourd derives from the capture of Inabayama, where the samurai under Hideyoshi's command waved spears with gourds tied to them as a signal. However, contemporary illustrations invariably show Hideyoshi's standard as consisting of one gourd only.

Oda or the Asai was by no means clear cut. Thus arrayed, the three greatest names in early modern Japanese history took part in the battle of Anegawa in 1570. This turned out to be a classic samurai encounter that began early in the morning of a hot summer's day across the shallow waters of the Anegawa (the Ane River). Aided immensely by the allied army of Tokugawa Ieyasu, Nobunaga won a fine victory that helped him regain some of the momentum lost by the defection of Asai Nagamasa. But the hostile anti-Nobunaga alliance was by no means destroyed, and over the following year Nobunaga, with Hideyoshi now within his senior ranks, was called upon to fight many different enemies. Among these were the armies associated in some way with the Buddhist religion rather than a daimyo. Several Buddhist establishments maintained armies, the most formidable being the Ikko-ikki of the True Pure Land sect, who were to oppose Nobunaga for ten years from their headquarters in the fortified cathedral of Ishiyama Honganji, built where Osaka castle now stands. In September 1570 Nobunaga led an attack on fortresses just to the north of Osaka that were held by the Miyoshi, the family who had been involved in replacing the previous shogun. The Asakura and Asai were also involved, and being repulsed once again by Nobunaga took refuge within the ancient monastic complex on Mount Hiei to the north-east of Kyoto. Angered by the support offered for his enemies given he was so close to home, in 1571 Nobunaga attacked and burned Mount Hiei, utterly destroying this most important centre of Buddhist learning and culture in Japan. Hideyoshi does not appear to have been involved in this most notorious of all Nobunaga's

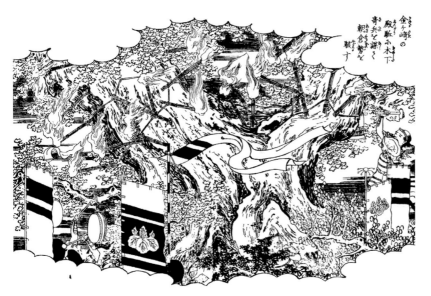

金ヶ崎の
殿を務め木下
藤吉郎と徳川勢と
朝倉勢を
観す

During his advance into Echizen province in 1570 Oda Nobunaga was told that his brother-in-law Asai Nagamasa had turned against him and was likely to cut off his retreat. A rapid strategic withdrawal was called for, and the dangerous task of providing the rearguard was taken by Hideyoshi and Tokugawa Ieyasu, the man who was later to oppose him. By their military skills Nobunaga's army withdrew to safety. This scene is from *Ehon Toyotomi Kunkoki*.

operations. We do know, however, that he was engaged against the Asai and Asakura in the operation that brought it about, because he wrote in a letter:

> We caught the Asai as they approached Kamaba Omote where we engaged them in battle. We cut into them and many were captured. I do not know how many were killed between Minouchi to Hachiman, but we waited for them at Hachiman in order to take a final revenge. We fought them three times, pursued them and destroyed them. We cut the heads off those who were killed and chased the others into the lake.

Nobunaga hoped to continue his war against the Asai and Asakura in 1572, but during that year he was forced to deal with an attempt by Takeda Shingen (1521–73), the formidable daimyo of central Japan, to break out from his mountainous location onto the Tokaido. This he did by defeating Nobunaga's ally Tokugawa Ieyasu at the battle of Mikata ga Hara. Three of Nobunaga's best generals were present at Mikata ga Hara. Toyotomi Hideyoshi was not there, having been given the job once again of keeping an eye on the Asai/Asakura front. The shogun Ashikaga Yoshiaki saw Shingen as a key supporter to help him break out of the stranglehold Nobunaga had put upon him, and Shingen's victory (which he failed to follow up because of the winter) encouraged Yoshiaki to challenge Nobunaga directly. He began to fortify his castle of Nijo within Kyoto and looked forward to the unfailing support of the anti-Nobunaga coalition. In one respect at least he was to be greatly disappointed, because the mighty Takeda Shingen received a bullet wound at the siege of Noda castle in 1573 and died shortly afterwards. So tragic was his death for the Takeda cause that his family tried to keep his death a secret, which succeeded at least with their own allies. Oda Nobunaga does not appear to have been fooled, and with this knowledge took the opportunity to depose Yoshiaki while the latter still believed Shingen was alive and would come to his rescue. Having disposed of the shogun, Nobunaga settled the matter of the Asai and Asakura once and for all a month later. In a dramatic move north Nobunaga managed to deal with the two armies separately, first destroying the Asakura at Ichijodani and then the Asai at their castle of Odani.

Although he is not named in the account, Toyotomi Hideyoshi may well have been present at the celebratory new year banquet that Nobunaga held in 1574 when the heads of the Asai and Asakura leaders were brought before him garishly lacquered in gold. Nevertheless, Hideyoshi was the main beneficiary of the destruction of the Asai, whom he had fought for several years. As a reward he was granted the former Asai territories in Omi province and their castle of Odani with an assessed income of 180,000 koku of rice (one koku was the theoretical amount needed to feed one man for one year). He was now a daimyo in Nobunaga's service, a position implying the typical combination of independence and trust that characterized Nobunaga's relationship with his closest followers. Such men were not required to pass on the taxes they collected to Nobunaga; they ruled their own provinces and enjoyed a certain degree of freedom in everything except for whom they should fight. Most of them were also moved from fief to fief as the years went by so that they did not acquire too much local support. That might have encouraged unseemly independent thinking.

When Hideyoshi took possession of Omi province in 1572 he changed his surname from Kinoshita to Hashiba, although the earlier name may have been a fabrication because his father probably had no surname at all. His given name of Hideyoshi dated from 1562. The new surname of Hashiba was formed from two characters taken from the names of two of Nobunaga's most illustrious generals: Ni(wa) Nagahide and (Shiba)ta Katsuie. Oda Nobunaga, however, continued to call him Saru (the monkey) in allusion to his alleged physical appearance.

Omi was strategically located in relation to Oda Nobunaga's own provinces, as Asai's defiance had shown, and one of Hideyoshi's first decisions was to transfer his capital from the mountain fortress of Odani to a site on the edge of Lake Biwa. This was a castle called Imahama, which Hideyoshi renamed Nagahama. Just like Nobunaga, he gathered around him in Omi

As a reward for his service against the Asai, Hideyoshi was given their former territories. This portrait of Hideyoshi as lord of the province hangs in the museum of Nagahama castle.

men he could trust, and was joined in Nagahama by his stepbrother Hashiba Hidenaga (1540–91) and four samurai leaders who were related to him by marriage. Also within his castle were some samurai from Owari who had joined him early in his career, and men from Mino who had passed under Oda control after the destruction of the Saito. All these were given parcels of land within Omi province from Hideyoshi's allocation. Once settled there he also gave employment to many former Asai retainers and copied Nobunaga in the creation of his own force of horse guards, each man being distinguished by the wearing of a yellow *horo*, the voluminous cloak on a bamboo framework that was traditionally the very visible mark of a valiant warrior.

During 1574 Nobunaga directed his efforts against the secondary Ikko-ikki stronghold of Nagashima, while 1575 finds Toyotomi Hideyoshi again commanding a contingent at a major Oda battle. This was the famous battle of Nagashino in 1575, which came about when Takeda Shingen's heir Katsuyori laid siege to the castle of Nagashino. Nobunaga marched to its rescue, but instead of falling onto the rear ranks of the Takeda siege lines he drew up his army some distance away on ground of his own choosing. The great strength of the Takeda had always lain in mounted warfare, so Nobunaga erected a loose palisade and lined up at least 1,000 arquebusiers, whose controlled fire broke the impact of a series of charges by the Takeda. Most of the fighting at Nagashino, however, was hand-to-hand combat, with Hideyoshi taking part in the command of a detached unit held back to deliver a counter-attack against the Takeda right flank.

Over the next five years Hashiba Hideyoshi and his fellow generals fought under Nobunaga's command in a series of operational theatres that resulted in the final collapse of the Takeda and the almost bloodless surrender of the Ikko-ikki's Ishiyama Honganji. The latter victory opened up the possibility of the expansion of Nobunaga's influence in a westerly direction for the first

Upon taking possession of the former Asai holdings, Hideyoshi realized that their former capital of Odani castle was poorly located compared with Imahama on Lake Biwa, so he built a castle there and renamed it Nagahama. This is the modern reconstruction of Nagahama's keep.

OPPOSITE:
The map shows the strategic position experienced by Hideyoshi as he made the transition from being Oda Nobunaga's leading general in 1577 to campaigning in his own right following Nobunaga's death in 1582. The coloured areas show the approximate boundaries during this time of the territories controlled by major daimyo and their allies, which changed somewhat over the period. For example, when the Takeda were defeated in 1582 the Tokugawa acquired Totomi, Suruga, Kai and Shinano to add to Mikawa. Hideyoshi's landholdings are included within those of Oda Nobunaga.

time, because along the shores of the Inland Sea the dominant power lay in the hands of the Mori family, whose naval expertise had sustained Ishiyama Honganji against Nobunaga's blockades. The conquest of this area was entrusted to Hashiba Hideyoshi, and towards the end of his life when he commissioned a biography Hideyoshi chose to see this campaign as the real beginning of his story.

THE HOUR OF DESTINY

Force and persuasion: from Himeji to Tottori 1577–81

Oda Nobunaga had been making plans as early as 1575 to take on the Mori, whose current daimyo, Mori Terumoto (1553–1625) represented one of the most formidable foes that Nobunaga would encounter in his entire career. The Mori territory not only included the Inland Sea with its myriad of tiny islands but stretched right across Honshu to the Sea of Japan and was defended to the east by sympathetic allies. This geographical spread helped determine Nobunaga's strategy and led him to commission two of his finest generals to advance along both of the two coastal routes. Akechi Mitsuhide (1526–82) proceeded north along the San'indo Road with an aim of attacking along the Sea of Japan coast through Wakasa and Tamba provinces. Hideyoshi was directed along the San'yodo Road towards the headquarters of Mori and his allies. Of the two campaigns, Akechi Mitsuhide met with the lesser success, and his campaign to pacify Tamba province became bogged down by stubborn resistance to his siege work and some profound differences of opinion with Nobunaga. Hideyoshi, by contrast, experienced slow but steady progress in a long operation that shows a maturity of technique and a readiness to embrace what came to be regarded as his hour of destiny. Chief among these techniques

Hideyoshi at his hour of destiny, 1577–82

Territories

- Mori & allies
- Otomo
- Shimazu
- Chosokabe
- Oda
- Uesugi
- Takeda
- Tokugawa
- Hojo

HOKKAIDO

SEA OF JAPAN

MUTSU

DEWA

SADO

ECHIGO

OKI

NOTO

ETCHU

KAGA

SHINANO

KOZUKE

SHIMOTSUKE

HITACHI

TAJIMA

WAKASA

Kita no sho

HIDA

MUSASHI

Tottori

TANGO

ECHIZEN

MINO

KAI

Edo (Tokyo)

SHIMOSA

IZUMO

HOKI

INABA

Yamazaki

Kyoto

Nagahama

Gifu

SAGAMI

KAZUSA

IWAMI

BINGO

MIMASAKA

HARIMA

TAMBA

YAMASHIRO

OMI

SURUGA

Odawara

AWA

Takamatsu

BITCHU

BIZEN

Himeji

SETTSU

IGA

MIKAWA

Nakamura

IZU

AKI

Osaka

OWARI

Nagashino

NAGATO

SUO

SANUKI

AWAJI

IZUMI

ISE

TOTOMI

HONSHU

Yamaguchi

CHIKIZEN

BUZEN

IYO

AWA

YAMATO

SHIMA

TSUSHIMA

HIZEN

CHIKUGO

TOSA

KAWACHI

KII

Nagasaki

BUNGO

SHIKOKU

GOTO
ISLANDS

HIGO

SATSUMA

HYUGA

Kagoshima

OSUMI

KYUSHU

PACIFIC OCEAN

TANEGASHIMA

N

| 0 | | 150 miles |
| 0 | | 150km |

were Hideyoshi's skills in siegecraft and negotiation, two means to an end that any successful besieger could and should combine as one, and this is what we find demonstrated over a long campaign that lasted from 1577 to 1582.

The modern traveller heading west from Osaka on the bullet train follows quite closely the route that Hideyoshi was to take along the sea coast through Himeji and Okayama. Himeji in Harima province was the first castle Hideyoshi had to face. It was then

In his later years, when he commissioned a biography, Hideyoshi identified his campaign to extend Nobunaga's domain to the west as the real beginning of his rise to greatness. Here we see Oda Nobunaga watching as Hideyoshi's army proceeds on its fateful journey. This scene is from *Ehon Toyotomi Kunkoki*.

called Himeyama, and as the finest survivor of the old Japanese castles Himeji is one of Japan's most popular tourist sites today. It lay where the San'yodo highway intersected with two other key roads, and its castellan was a certain Kodera Masamoto, whose loyalties to the Mori were somewhat unsure. Fortunately for Hideyoshi there was also present in Himeji a man called Kuroda Yoshitaka (1546–1604) who had married Masamoto's daughter and had temporarily assumed the surname of Kodera. Kuroda Yoshitaka made contact with Nobunaga through Hideyoshi, and explained the strategic position concisely. In Harima province there was only one other powerful daimyo: Bessho Nagaharu (1558–80) of Miki castle, and if the Kodera were to ally themselves with Nobunaga's cause then smaller families locally would follow them, putting the new alliance in a good position to take Miki. Overcoming any further resistance, he said, would then be 'like splitting bamboo'. So through the mediation of Kuroda Yoshitaka, which was backed up in the conventional way by the sending of Yoshitaka's ten-year-old son

The key to taking Harima province was Miki castle, controlled by Bessho Nagaharu. Hideyoshi first acquired Himeji, and used it as a base to overcome Miki, which is shown here, after a long campaign. This scene is from *Ehon Toyotomi Kunkoki*.

Kuroda Nagamasa to Nobunaga as a hostage, Yoshitaka's father-in-law was persuaded to surrender Himeji to Hideyoshi without a shot being fired. A crucial castle had therefore been gained, and with it another samurai whose loyalty to Hideyoshi was to last until the end of his life. The young hostage Kuroda Nagamasa (1568–1623) would one day lead a division of Hideyoshi's army in the invasion of Korea.

The next tower to topple was indeed Miki, although it took much longer than anticipated. Hideyoshi wished to spare Bessho Nagaharu so that he might join the Oda side as well, and the siege was pressed forward on Hideyoshi's behalf by the loyal Kodera and Kuroda lords. Not every element of Hideyoshi's carefully considered plans worked. He did indeed win Miki castle, but Bessho Nagaharu preferred to commit suicide rather than submit, and at the same time Hideyoshi had to deal with a problem to his rear. Araki Murashige had submitted to Nobunaga in 1573. His demonstration of loyalty to Nobunaga, supposedly proven by being made to eat *manju* (bean jam buns) off the sharp point of Nobunaga's sword, had earned him the castle of Itami. Murashige's behaviour came under suspicion while Hideyoshi was undertaking his campaign along the San'yodo, and, believing that he was about to be attacked, Murashige shut himself in his castle. The Kodera and Kuroda moved against him during the Miki operation, as shown by a letter from Hideyoshi that states: 'As far as [the lord of] Itami is concerned, it seems to me it will be defeated in three to five days because you have filled the moat in so quickly.' Hideyoshi was incorrect in the time it took to subdue him, and Murashige withstood a year-long siege before managing to escape and join the Mori.

A similarly successful combination of force and persuasion prevailed when Hideyoshi advanced into Bizen province and took on the Ukita family. Ukita Naoie (1530–81) owed the Mori a great debt, because it had been owing to Mori support that he had been able to overcome his own daimyo Urakami Munekage and seize Bizen province for himself in 1577. Taking his cue from the example of Nobunaga, Ukita Naoie had concentrated his power in the strategically placed Okayama castle with a few satellites instead of a string of smaller mountain fortresses. In 1578 the Mori forces confronted Hideyoshi in battle at Kozuki, a castle held for Oda Nobunaga by the Amako family who were bitter enemies of the Mori. Ukita Naoie sensed that the Mori would fail against Nobunaga's advance, and sent only a token force to aid the Mori, pleading personal illness in mitigation. The approach paid off, and when Ukita Naoie died in 1581 his domain was confirmed by Oda Nobunaga as being the inheritance of his young son Ukita Hideie, whom Hideyoshi adopted.

Oda Nobunaga has gone down in history as a commander who dealt savagely with opponents, although Hideyoshi himself knew how to be ruthless when circumstances dictated. Probably the cruellest of Hideyoshi's campaigns was the 200-day siege of Tottori castle in Inaba province, where the defenders are believed to have resorted to cannibalism. This scene is from *Ehon Taikoki*, an illustrated life of Hideyoshi with woodblock illustrations by Okada Gyokuzan.

Early in 1580 Hideyoshi was granted the two provinces of Harima and Tajima as his fief and made Himeji his new headquarters. Nagahama castle was transferred to another of Nobunaga's generals, thus demonstrating that none was totally free in his fief but that all were dependent upon the needs and wishes of Nobunaga. With Himeji as his base Hideyoshi's campaign against the Mori could become more ambitious, and later that year he headed north and entered Inaba province on the Sea of Japan, where a sprawling mountain fortress called Tottori was in the hands of Yamana Toyokuni. Mori Terumoto sent Kikkawa Tsuneie to Tottori with reinforcements, at which Toyokuni abandoned his responsibilities and fled. Tsuneie, however, resolved to withstand any attack, and the stage was set for one of the most bitter of all Hideyoshi's operations. All attempts at negotiation were turned down, so Hideyoshi drove the local villagers into the castle and encircled Tottori in a tight blockade. The siege of Itami had lasted for a whole year largely because the besieging forces failed to prevent supplies and reinforcements from arriving. At Tottori Hideyoshi left no margin of error in this regard and took personal charge of the siege, where he demonstrated an element of ruthlessness and cruelty that is usually a charge placed against his master Oda Nobunaga. Towers were placed every 500m or so round the perimeter, and Hideyoshi waited for the garrison literally to die of starvation. To aid the process he bought up all the available rice in Inaba province at several times the market price. Over a period of 200 days the defenders were reduced to eating dead horses, grass and finally, it is believed, turned to cannibalism with the corpses of their dead comrades. Any emaciated occupants who tried to flee were picked off by Hideyoshi's arquebusiers. Eventually Tsuneie agreed to surrender, one of the conditions being his own suicide. He wrote to his son: 'We have endured for over two hundred days. We now have no provisions left. It is my belief that by giving up my life I will help my garrison. There is nothing greater than the honour of our family.'

Shimizu Muneharu was the commander of Takamatsu castle in Bitchu province. Hideyoshi's dramatic siege of Takamatsu proved to be the turning point in his career. This portrait of Shimizu Muneharu is in the Memorial Hall on the site of the castle.

After a brief visit to Nobunaga at the lunar new year Hideyoshi returned to Himeji to put the finishing touches to a plan whereby the year 1582 would see him moving farther westwards along the San'yodo through Ukita Hideie's friendly Bizen province and into hostile Bitchu, where, not far over the provincial border from Okayama, stood the castle of Takamatsu, which is usually referred to as Bitchu-Takamatsu to distinguish it from a castle with the same name on Shikoku Island. It was to provide the dramatic background to the moment when Hideyoshi's life changed for ever.

With water and the flood: Bitchu-Takamatsu 1582

The first weapon Hideyoshi brought to bear against Bitchu-Takamatsu was negotiation, backed up by an attempt to bribe the commander, Shimizu Muneharu

(1537–82). It was a generous offer. If Muneharu betrayed the Mori and handed over Takamatsu castle the whole of Bitchu province would be his, but Muneharu refused and prepared for a siege. As a satellite castle of the Mori, Takamatsu lay in a favourable position, situated on a modest patch of relatively high ground in the middle of a wide flat plain. Wooded mountains surrounded it on three sides, but they were at too far a distance to be used as conventional siege positions, so its lines of communication could not be easily controlled as at Tottori. Instead, any besieging army would have to construct siege lines in the flat fields under the sight and range of the castle's walls. To the west flowed a river, the Ashinorigawa, which was also useful for keeping any besieging force at a distance.

What Hideyoshi did was to turn each of these features to his own advantage. The fall of the land towards the east was slight, but sufficient to allow the river to flood the castle if its flow could be diverted. So Hideyoshi

The small clump of trees in front of the hill on the right of this picture shows the remains of the dyke built by Hideyoshi to flood Takamatsu castle. The castle site is about a kilometre beyond the large *torii* gate.

The siege and flooding of Bitchu-Takamatsu castle, 1582

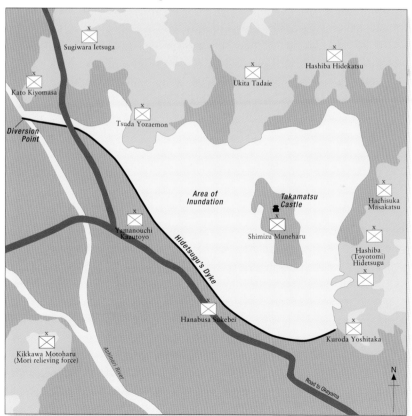

The site of Bitchu-Takamatsu castle, which lay only a few metres above sea level, is shown isolated by the artificial lake formed by the diversion of the Ashinori River. Hideyoshi's army is shown in positions on the surrounding hills, while a relieving army under Kikkawa Motoharu stands helplessly on a hill to the south. The numbers on both sides are unfortunately not known, but Hideyoshi's force was certainly very considerable, because it denuded Oda Nobunaga of protection, a factor that led to his death.

gave orders for a dyke to be built that was anchored on the first hill to the east beyond the castle. A small portion of it has survived to this day and has been preserved by the local council. The dyke then curved round Takamatsu for 2.8km, damming the Ashinorigawa at a point almost due west of the fortress. This dyke was no mere wooden fence or palisade, but a reinforced earthwork made from straw bags full of earth piled solidly together (probably using a wooden frame) to make a wall with a trapezoidal cross section. It measured approximately 22m at its base and 11m at the top, with a height of 7.3m. Thousands of labourers were fed and paid to build it over a furious period of 12 days. The rainy season then helped the river to overflow its banks beside the dyke, and gradually the water accumulated to make an artificial lake that lapped against the top of the dyke at its eastern lower side and faded to nothing at its higher western end. But the castle of Takamatsu lay in the middle, and as the waters rose around its walls Shimizu Muneharu's contact with the outside world gradually disappeared under the flood waters. Hideyoshi's generals took up positions on the hills while the discomfort of the garrison was increased by boats that made their way under the walls to deliver volleys of bullets.

Yet still Shimizu Muneharu would not surrender. By now Mori Terumoto had been apprised of the situation and guessed that Hideyoshi's legendary stubbornness would not permit him to abandon the objective Nobunaga had set him when all he needed was time. Tottori, after all, had held out for 200 days, but unlike Tottori, Bitchu-Takamatsu was within easy reach of the Mori heartlands. The flooding technique and the creation of the artificial lake may have increased the risk of starvation, but it had also placed Hideyoshi in an unenviable position should Mori Terumoto decide to attempt a relief. Hideyoshi's units were scattered around on the hills, and if Mori attacked him Hideyoshi could well be forced to fight with his lake at his back. On receiving intelligence that Mori Terumoto was indeed preparing such a move Hideyoshi sent a messenger to Nobunaga informing him of the situation and requesting urgent reinforcements.

The news reached Oda Nobunaga at a time of great personal happiness. He had just returned from the mountains of Shinano province in central Japan, where his son and heir Oda Nobutada (1557–82), ably assisted by Tokugawa Ieyasu, had finally put paid to the Takeda. Takeda Katsuyori, defeated at Nagashino, had held out for seven years. His death at the battle of Temmokuzan meant that Nobunaga was now secure in the east, and had made him so confident of his continuing success that he was now planning his next move: an ambitious conquest of the island of Shikoku to be led by Nobutada. On the assumption that Hideyoshi was heading for victory against the Mori, an invasion of Shikoku across the Inland Sea would meet with little hindrance, so Nobunaga even went to the extent of parcelling out the territory of Shikoku as rewards before any move had even been made.

Hideyoshi's urgent request for reinforcements against the Mori was taken by the triumphant Oda Nobunaga as good news rather than bad, because Nobunaga realized that Hideyoshi's siege of Takamatsu had finally drawn

Mori Terumoto into the open. It was the perfect opportunity for a showdown, and a victorious battle would be of such far-reaching consequence that Nobunaga decided to lead the army in person. As Hideyoshi's need for help was pressing Nobunaga arranged for certain of his generals to go on ahead of him. The most important among them was Akechi Mitsuhide, whose San'indo campaign may have been modest in its gains but had earned for him the castle of Kameyama in Tamba province. Tamba-Kameyama lay to the west of Kyoto, so it made sense for Nobunaga to dispatch Mitsuhide back to his home castle with all haste in order to lead an army to aid Hideyoshi. While Mitsuhide did this Nobunaga also moved west from Azuchi to Kyoto to stay the night at the Nichiren sect's Honnoji temple, meaning to follow the next morning. But Akechi Mitsuhide did not continue on his march to the west. Instead his bemused and mystified men received orders to head back to Kyoto, where, unknown to them, Mitsuhide planned to launch them in a military coup against Nobunaga. His treacherous plot was hatched in such complete secrecy that he told his four leading captains about it only a few hours prior to moving. When his army of 13,000 men were ordered to set off in an easterly direction it was explained to them that they were going to be inspected by Nobunaga before leaving for battle, and they were ordered to attack the temple only when they neared the Honnoji compound. The surprise was total; Nobunaga heard a disturbance outside and thought that a brawl had broken out. His guards, pages and attendants were completely overwhelmed. Fighting bravely to the last, Nobunaga committed suicide. Intending a clean sweep of the Oda family, Akechi's army moved on to the nearby Myokakuji temple where Nobunaga's heir Oda Nobutada was staying and disposed of him in a similarly efficient manner.

Akechi's coup was a remarkable success. Both Nobunaga and his talented son had been surprised and killed, throwing Nobunaga's control of Japan into utter disarray partly because the remaining Oda heirs turned out to be confused, divided and impotent. Nobunaga's second son Oda Nobuo

This lively woodblock print shows Hideyoshi in charge of the flooding of Bitchu-Takamatsu. As the waters rise the defenders are bombarded from guns mounted on boats.

(1558–1630, whose name is often read as Nobukatsu) could have responded and avenged his father but he hesitated, while Nobunaga's third son Oda Nobutaka (1558–83) was in the harbour of Sakai ready to move against Shikoku as part of the planned invasion when the dreadful news reached him. His reaction was somewhat irrational. Believing that his cousin Nobuzumi (1555–82), who had married Mitsuhide's daughter, must have been in on the conspiracy, Nobutaka hurried to Osaka and had him murdered, while Mitsuhide himself was left alone. Tokugawa Ieyasu was probably the only man east of Kyoto who could respond in any meaningful way, but he had been visiting Nobunaga with a small retinue just before the Honnoji incident occurred and was separated from his army back in Okazaki. After a perilous journey home he finally assembled his forces and set off to confront the usurper, only to be told when he reached the vicinity of modern Nagoya that there was no longer any need of his services. Akechi Mitsuhide was dead, and Oda Nobunaga had been avenged by his faithful follower Toyotomi Hideyoshi.

Showdown at Yamazaki, 1582

Among the many calculations that Akechi Mitsuhide must have made before launching his audacious coup was the fairly safe bet that Toyotomi

Hideyoshi in command, Yamazaki 1582

It is the night before the battle of Yamazaki in 1582. Hideyoshi's army has completed a forced march from Bitchu-Takamatsu castle in order to engage with the usurper Akechi Mitsuhide, and in the vicinity of the village of Yamazaki Hideyoshi discusses with his leading officers the plan that will soon be put into operation. His headquarters post is far from elaborate and consists of no more than the open rectangle formed by *maku*, upon which are emblazoned Hideyoshi's *mon* of a paulownia design. His security is assured not by any wall or fence but by the human wall of his horse guards, who are presently dismounted and stand in attendance at his rear. Each wears a *horo*, the ornamental cloak that was stretched over a light bamboo framework and billowed out when the guardsman galloped along. These elite samurai are organized in two guards units distinguished by a red or a yellow *horo*. The colour yellow also predominates in Hideyoshi's own flags. In pride of place is Hideyoshi's *o uma jirushi* (great standard) of a golden gourd from which is suspended an additional yellow flag. His *ko uma jirushi* (lesser standard) is a large red fan with a golden streamer beneath it. Just outside the *maku* we see a line of tall yellow *nobori* banners with slashed edges. These would be used en masse to deliver visual signals to units out in the field. A similar but smaller flag is worn on the back of the armour of one of Hideyoshi's courier guards, who kneels before him ready to convey a written or verbal message to other units on the battlefield. The great general Toyotomi Hideyoshi himself is dressed in a fine suit of armour beneath a *jinbaori*, set off by a magnificent black helmet with a sunburst rear crest, an allusion to the legend that Hideyoshi was conceived when a burst of sunlight shone upon his mother. He holds a war fan covered in red silk and ornamented with pearls that is now owned by Osaka Castle Museum, where there is also a replica of the helmet. His *bugyo* (staff officers) are more simply attired as they pore over the map of Yamazaki that is spread out before them on a makeshift table created from a portable wooden shield.

In a dramatic twist of fate Hideyoshi intercepted the messenger sent to the Mori with the news of Nobunaga's death. Keeping it a secret he negotiated the surrender of Takamatsu castle, one of the conditions being the suicide of Shimizu Muneharu. This the brave commander performed in grand style in a boat on the artificial lake. This picture is in the Memorial Museum on the site of the castle.

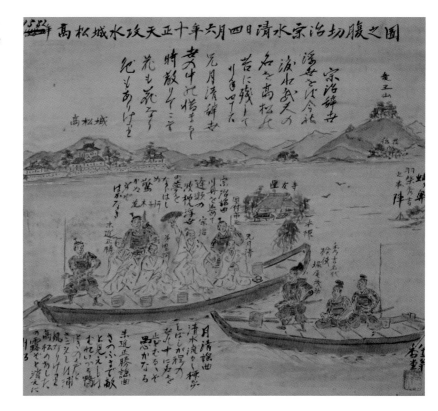

Hideyoshi would be unable to react because any abandonment of the siege of Takamatsu would be interrupted by Mori Terumoto falling on his rear. To ensure that this was a certainty Mitsuhide sent a messenger to Mori Terumoto as soon as Nobunaga was dead, promising him great things if he would now obligingly finish off Hideyoshi in the sure knowledge that no other army flying the Oda flag would be heading against him. In a dramatic stroke of fate the messenger was intercepted on his way by Hideyoshi, who immediately summoned Ankokuji Ekei, the Mori's chief negotiator, to his presence. The concessions Hideyoshi was willing to make to bring the siege of Takamatsu to a close were quite considerable. To Ekei it appeared that Hideyoshi was very worried about the power of the Mori, but he, of course, had no idea about what had just happened in Kyoto. Hideyoshi offered to end the fighting and leave nearly all the Mori territories intact in return for the cession to Nobunaga of the provinces of Hoki, Mimasaka and Bitchu. Ankokuji Ekei considered the offer carefully, reckoning that Mimasaka had virtually passed into Nobunaga's control anyway; that the fall of Hoki was only a matter of time and that Bitchu could be abandoned, so he recommended this course of action to Mori Terumoto. The only other condition was the suicide of Shimizu Muneharu. This the brave defender of Takamatsu castle performed in grand style, cutting his belly in an open boat out on the artificial lake that Hideyoshi had created.

It was not long before Mori Terumoto heard what lay behind Hideyoshi's urgent concessions. He could have fallen on Hideyoshi's army there and then as the latter prepared to march back to Kyoto, but something held him back. He may well have been urged towards this course of action by Ankokuji Ekei and Kobayakawa Takakage, two men who were well respected within the Mori household and both of whom were to prosper in the future under Hideyoshi. Nevertheless, to allow Hideyoshi the doubtful privilege of overcoming Akechi Mitsuhide on everyone else's behalf may have seemed like a very good idea.

For Hideyoshi to succeed against Akechi Mitsuhide speed was of the essence, because for the past 11 days Mitsuhide had reigned unchallenged. The imperial court (under pressure) had sent him its congratulations, and he had behaved like a liberator in Kyoto by declaring exemptions from taxes and making shrewd donations, so the longer he behaved like a hero who had removed a dictator then the more likely it was that others would rally to his flag. Fortunately for Hideyoshi his own castle of Himeji lay halfway to Kyoto, so his return was far from being a dangerous journey across enemy territory. On 25 June Hideyoshi led his army in a forced march of 12km from Takamatsu to Numa, where they stayed the night. Early on 26 June they began a 40km march farther on to Himeji, where he rested and reviewed his position on 27 June. On the morning of 28 June he left Himeji, and with one more overnight stop reached Amagasaki, following the coast of the Inland Sea for a total of 80km. As he passed through Osaka, Hideyoshi was joined by Niwa Nagahide, another of Nobunaga's generals, and Oda Nobutaka. Having Nobutaka ride with him was an enormous boost for Hideyoshi because the presence of one of Nobunaga's sons gave him an additional legitimacy to proceed.

The news of Hideyoshi's approach reached Akechi Mitsuhide on 29 June. His ability to hinder any hostile approach against Kyoto was quite considerable, because he controlled two castles (Shoryuji and Yodo) that covered the approaches to Kyoto from either side of the Yodogawa. These fortresses lay just to the north of the narrow neck of land through which all the railway lines between Osaka and Kyoto now pass. As Hideyoshi's army was large Mitsuhide had no desire to be caught inside either castle with his force divided, so he took up a position near the village of Yamazaki and stationed his army behind the small Enmyojigawa, which entered the Yodogawa to the north of the village and provided an excellent defensive line.

As he drew near to Yamazaki Hideyoshi realized that the key to the battle was a 270m-high wooded hill called Tennozan, which lay beside Yamazaki and completely dominated the road to Kyoto. He therefore sent a detachment under Nakagawa Kiyohide to secure the heights, which

After settling the surrender of Bitchu-Takamatsu, Hideyoshi hurried back to Kyoto and met the usurper Akechi Mitsuhide in battle at Yamazaki. Hideyoshi's men occupied Tennozan, the mountain that overlooked the Akechi positions. When the battle started a fierce contest to regain Tennozan began. Here we see Matsuda Masachika being killed by Hideyoshi's samurai on a mountain path. This scene is from *Ehon Toyotomi Kunkoki*.

Hideyoshi's rise to power, 1582–85

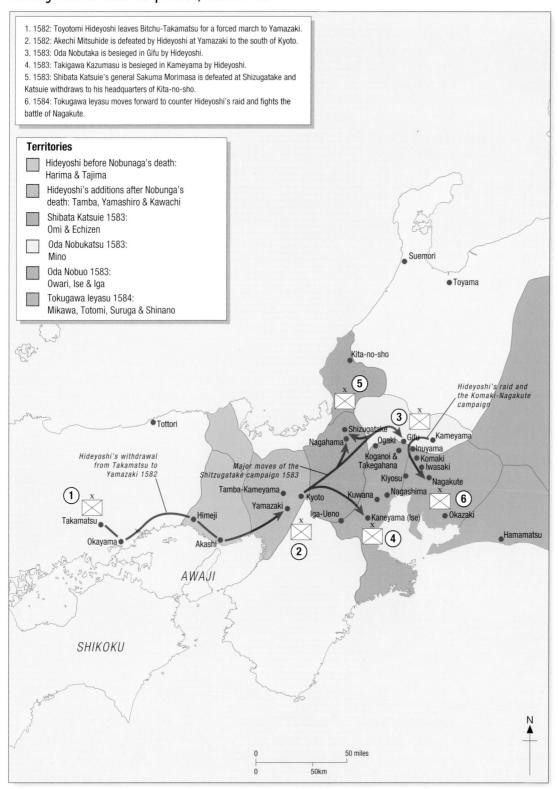

1. 1582: Toyotomi Hideyoshi leaves Bitchu-Takamatsu for a forced march to Yamazaki.
2. 1582: Akechi Mitsuhide is defeated by Hideyoshi at Yamazaki to the south of Kyoto.
3. 1583: Oda Nobutaka is besieged in Gifu by Hideyoshi.
4. 1583: Takigawa Kazumasu is besieged in Kameyama by Hideyoshi.
5. 1583: Shibata Katsuie's general Sakuma Morimasa is defeated at Shizugatake and Katsuie withdraws to his headquarters of Kita-no-sho.
6. 1584: Tokugawa Ieyasu moves forward to counter Hideyoshi's raid and fights the battle of Nagakute.

Territories

- Hideyoshi before Nobunaga's death: Harima & Tajima
- Hideyoshi's additions after Nobunga's death: Tamba, Yamashiro & Kawachi
- Shibata Katsuie 1583: Omi & Echizen
- Oda Nobukatsu 1583: Mino
- Oda Nobuo 1583: Owari, Ise & Iga
- Tokugawa Ieyasu 1584: Mikawa, Totomi, Suruga & Shinano

Suemori

Toyama

Kita-no-sho

Hideyoshi's raid and the Komaki-Nagakute campaign

Tottori

Shizugatake
Nagahama
Ogaki
Gifu
Kameyama
Inuyama
Koganoi & Takegahana
Komaki
Iwasaki
Kiyosu
Hideyoshi's withdrawal from Takamatsu to Yamazaki 1582
Major moves of the Shitzugatake campaign 1583
Tamba-Kameyama
Yamazaki
Kyoto
Kuwana
Nagashima
Nagakute
Takamatsu
Himeji
Iga-Ueno
Okazaki
Okayama
Akashi
Kaneyama (Ise)
Hamamatsu

AWAJI

SHIKOKU

N

| 0 | 50 miles |
| 0 | 50km |

28

established his presence in the area and covered his own movements. On the night of 1 July two of Hideyoshi's generals, Nakamura Kazuuji and Horio Yoshiharu, sent ninja into the Akechi camp, where they set fire to abandoned buildings and generally caused confusion. Nakagawa Mitsuhide was replaced on Tennozan by other troops and took up his own position on the Hashiba left flank.

On the morning of 2 July Hideyoshi's army moved forward to confront the Akechi force across the Enmyojigawa while a fierce battle began for the control of Tennozan. Mitsuhide's samurai under Matsuda Masachika and Nabika Kamon attempted to fight their way up the paths, but were driven back by arquebus fire with many casualties. With the dominance of Tennozan thus assured, Hideyoshi sent his right wing across the Enmyojigawa to perform an encircling movement. In spite of fierce resistance they managed to penetrate the forward troops, and turned towards the Akechi main body. At this Hideyoshi committed his left wing from upstream, who were supported by a fierce surge from the troops on Tennozan. The impetus was too much for the Akechi army, who broke and ran, except for the brave Mimaki Kaneaki, who charged forward with only 200 soldiers and was engulfed in the sea of Hideyoshi's army. As the Akechi army retreated, the panic spread back even to Akechi Mitsuhide's own bodyguard. The garrison of Shoryuji castle collapsed as Hideyoshi's army continued a vigorous pursuit, and Mitsuhide fled for his life. He made it only as far as a village called Ogurusu, where he fell victim to a gang of bandits, the sort usually attracted to battlefields, who preyed upon wounded samurai. Their leader thrust a spear at him from within the protection of a bamboo grove, and he fell dead from his horse, 13 days after accomplishing the death of Oda Nobunaga.

The destruction of Akechi Mitsuhide at Yamazaki gave Hideyoshi great moral influence among the other former generals of Nobunaga. His master stroke was to convince them to recognize Nobunaga's infant grandson Samboshi as heir, thus dividing the supporters of Nobunaga's brothers Nobuo and Nobutaka.

A house divided: Shizugatake, 1583

The decisive battle of Yamazaki left a power vacuum that Hideyoshi was determined to fill, and the process began one month after Nobunaga's death when nearly all the men who had once been his vassals gathered at Kiyosu castle. Two important items were on their agenda. The first was the redistribution of the recently conquered territories. The second, and of infinitely greater importance, was the selection of an heir to whom they could swear loyalty. Shibata Katsuie (1530–83) favoured Nobunaga's third son Oda Nobutaka, whose presence at Yamazaki beside Hideyoshi had served to wipe away memories of the murder of his cousin and had made him the natural leader in many eyes. Katsuie's opinion was of great importance, because he had been Nobunaga's senior councillor for many years. Within the Oda army organization he had held command over all units, except those consisting of Oda family members, which had made him the lowly Hideyoshi's commander. Others preferred Oda Nobuo, the second son of Nobunaga and heir by

primogeniture, but Hideyoshi, whose position as the avenger of Nobunaga when all others had hesitated had given him great moral influence, entered the room bearing in his arms Samboshi, Nobunaga's three-year-old grandson.

The conference agreed to recognize Samboshi as Nobunaga's heir and appoint Nobutaka as his guardian. Hideyoshi had pulled off another master stroke. His own choice for heir, an infant but arguably the true heir of his grandfather, had been selected, while the boy's two uncles were exposed as potential rivals. In the months that followed, any genuine enmity that existed between Nobutaka and Nobuo was to be ruthlessly inflated and exploited to serve other people's ends.

Hideyoshi then proceeded to establish a strong personal presence in Kyoto and built a new castle at Yamazaki. He then waited for some provocation, and it was Oda Nobutaka who came most splendidly to his aid. As earnest of his alliance with Shibata Katsuie, Nobutaka's aunt Oichi (the widow of Asai Nagamasa) was married off to Katsuie, and by the winter of 1582 a league of Nobunaga's former generals who believed that Hideyoshi was planning to take over his former domains was beginning to take shape. Had they formed a clear and firm alliance and then acted in a coordinated manner they might have been able to prevent that which they suspected and feared. Instead their response to Hideyoshi was isolated and sporadic, and Hideyoshi, who had shown at Yamazaki that he was the master of movement, was able to pick them off one by one. That he managed to do this was quite extraordinary, because his opponents were ranged against him over nearly all the points of the compass except the west where he had reached accommodation with the Mori. Oda Nobutaka dominated the Nakasendo to the north-east from mighty Gifu. Farther north still was Shibata Katsuie, who could march on Kyoto from Kita-no-sho (modern Fukui) in Echizen province. His son Katsutoyo held Hideyoshi's former possession of Nagahama, while another anti-Hideyoshi general, Takigawa Kazumasu, was located at the fortress of Nagashima on the Pacific coast.

Fortunately for Hideyoshi, Oda Nobutaka foolishly decided to break ranks and make a hostile move against Hideyoshi before the snow had melted in the Echizen mountain passes, which meant that his mentor Shibata Katsuie could not move to help him. Fully appreciating this point, Hideyoshi moved rapidly against Gifu, and such was his reputation for successful siege work that Nobutaka immediately surrendered when the army arrived. Acting with considerable generosity, Hideyoshi allowed Nobutaka to remain in Gifu in return for a pledge of loyalty. On arriving back in Kyoto, Hideyoshi learned that Takigawa Kazumasu in Kameyama had also

Heavy snow during the winter of 1582/83 gave Hideyoshi the opportunity to consolidate his position in Kyoto uninterrupted by any threat from his main rival Shibata Katsuie, whose approach to Kyoto was through mountain passes blocked with snow. Here we see labourers sent by Katsuie attempting to clear the way to Gifu castle, held by Oda Nobutaka, another of Hideyoshi's potential enemies. This scene is from *Ehon Toyotomi Kunkoki*.

begun to move and was planning a two-pronged attack in conjunction with Shibata Katsutoyo, whose position on the eastern shore of Lake Biwa was unaffected by the winter weather. Hideyoshi first marched to Nagahama and bought its surrender with a large bribe. He then turned on Takigawa Kazumasu in Kameyama and conducted the first successful siege of a Japanese castle involving the use of mines to collapse a section of wall. Spring was now on its way, and the thaw would free Shibata Katsuie from his frozen fastness. To guard against this Hideyoshi sent several detachments of troops north of Lake Biwa to strengthen the existing garrisons of the mountaintop forts that covered the Hokkokukaido highway to the north.

This statue of a sleeping soldier provides a memorial to the battle of Shizugatake in 1583. It stands on the highest point of the mountain ridge along which the battle was fought.

When spring came and the snow in the Echizen passes melted away, Shibata Katsuie led his army south and, just as Hideyoshi had expected, the fortress line provided a genuine barrier, so Katsuie set up his positions on other mountains opposite. The two front lines were now separated by just under 5km, with the mountain peak of Tenjin and its adjacent valleys acting as a no man's land between them. The northern army totalled about 20,000 men.

Hideyoshi then marched north to join his frontier force, but no sooner did he arrive at Kinomoto, the nearest town to the fortress line, than he had to leave to face a serious threat to his rear. Having heard of the developments, Oda Nobutaka in Gifu, whom Hideyoshi had generously allowed to retain possession both of the castle and his own head, regretted his earlier surrender and threw his weight behind Shibata Katsuie, who had always supported his claim. Hideyoshi was therefore forced to march back along the Nakasendo with 20,000 men to besiege Gifu once again, but he wisely based himself in the nearby fortress on Ogaki, which lay on the same road, just in case Shibata Katsuie should break through in the north. This second assault on Gifu was cleverly delegated to Oda Nobuo, who had been convinced by Hideyoshi that his 'treacherous' younger brother was the main obstacle to his receiving his just inheritance. Hideyoshi left on 17 April, and Nobuo started the attack on Gifu early on 19 April.

Shortly after Hideyoshi's departure Shibata Katsuie began an operation to capture the frontier forts. It was led by Sakuma Morimasa, whose initial tactics were very clever, because he concentrated on the forts to the west of the road, which contained the weakest garrisons. With Maeda Toshiie providing a rearguard, and masking the minor outposts to their left, the assaults concentrated first on Oiwa and then on Iwasaki by circling round to the west of Lake Yogo. This allowed his men to advance against them from the south-west along the mountain ridge, rather than by a frontal assault from the more difficult northern side. The garrison at Shizugatake, the next fort along the ridge, did not dare sally out to challenge them. The forts across the valley were now perilously isolated and they were to be the next target. Then, with all the peaks secured, Hideyoshi's rearguard down in the valley under Hashiba Hidenaga could be wiped out and the mountain pass would be secure.

This is the view from the summit of Shizugatake looking north along the ridge.

At first all went well. Oiwa was the first to fall, and its commander Nakagawa Kiyohide was killed. Iwasaki fell soon afterwards after an attack along the ridge from the south, but its commander Takayama Ukon escaped across the Hokkokukaido to Tagami. Apart from the two smaller forward positions, Sakuma now occupied all of Hideyoshi's castles west of the road except for Shizugatake, upon which he could now concentrate all his forces. Having been forced to watch his two comrades along the ridge lose their castles, Kuwayama Shigeharu and his 1,000 men in Shizugatake must have been very apprehensive about their fate. Yet it does not seem to have diminished their fighting spirit, nor was there any question of surrender.

On the other side, Shibata Katsuie became more concerned with every hour that passed over the evidence that messengers brought to him about how dangerously vulnerable Sakuma Morimasa was to a counter-attack. Hashiba Hidenaga, after all, was only just across the valley with 15,000 men, and Shibata also knew that another of Hideyoshi's allies, Niwa Nagahide, was not too far away on Lake Biwa with 2,000 men. There was also the question of Toyotomi Hideyoshi himself, but by all accounts he and his 20,000-strong army were every bit as engrossed with the siege of Gifu as Sakuma was with the siege of Shizugatake. Nevertheless, the prudent Shibata Katsuie sent a messenger to Sakuma Morimasa ordering him to abandon his open siege lines for the security of the newly captured Oiwa castle. Sakuma Morimasa pooh-poohed the idea. Shizugatake would be his before night fell, and he dismissed out of hand any suggestion that Hideyoshi could return to its relief when he was entangled with Gifu.

By now a messenger had galloped to Ogaki with the intelligence for Hideyoshi that Oiwa and Iwasaki had fallen and that Shizugatake was likely to follow. When asked if Sakuma had withdrawn into Oiwa the messenger replied that he had not. At this moment, according to Hideyoshi's admiring biographer, his expression changed from sorrow to one of glee. 'Then I have won!' Hideyoshi is said to have exclaimed. His long military experience had told him that Sakuma Morimasa was dangerously exposed. The spontaneity of the Yamazaki campaign had to be revisited.

Very early on the morning of 20 April 1583 Toyotomi Hideyoshi made ready to rush back to Kinomoto. He left 5,000 men under Oda Nobuo to continue the siege of Gifu and began the great gamble. The only way he could achieve surprise was by taking a largely mounted army with him while the infantry and supplies marched along far behind. It was an enormous risk to separate the different units of his army in this way, but it was a chance that Hideyoshi had to take. Burning pine torches lit their way as Hideyoshi's army of 1,000 mounted samurai and their exhausted personal attendants hurried along the familiar and well-trodden road. The main body of 15,000 men brought up the rear, but the gap between the two lengthened with every second. From Ogaki the ride took them through Sekigahara, a village whose name was to become very familiar 20 years later, and on to Kinomoto, which they reached in an unbelievable five hours after leaving Ogaki. The first that Sakuma Morimasa knew of their arrival was the sudden appearance of 1,000 burning pine torches down in the valley. Hideyoshi paused only to collect Hashiba Hidenaga's troops in Tagami and to be apprised of the situation. Then, following a signal from a conch shell trumpet blown, it is said, by Hideyoshi himself, his eager and impatient men poured up the mountain paths towards Shizugatake and Sakuma's siege lines.

Battles fought on the tops of mountains are not a common occurrence in military history. Even in a country like Japan, where mountains are plentiful and many have castles or the remains of them on their summits, mountaintop conflicts either tended to be sieges or consisted of actions fought in the valleys below, with the hilltops being used solely as vantage points. This is what makes Shizugatake almost unique. It was not a siege but a field engagement, except that the 'field' lay on the tops and along the ridges of a wooded mountain chain. It was also fought as the result of a surprise attack by night on an unsuspecting enemy. The twist here is that the army that was both surprised and defeated was the one that up until that point had been holding the high ground.

The first armed contact was made as dawn was breaking. All along the mountain paths and in among the trees numerous small-group and individual combats took place. There were no lines of well-drilled arquebusiers as at Nagashino. Instead a huge disjointed mêlée began, with Hideyoshi's horse guards playing a leading role. Spears, swords and daggers decided the outcome of Shizugatake, not blocks of spearmen, and the heroes of the hour were the seven valiant warriors named as 'The Seven Spears of Shizugatake', who were all members of Hideyoshi's

Leaving his other military actions in capable hands, Hideyoshi hurried to Shizugatake to take on Katsuie's disobedient general Sakuma Morimasa. This print by Yoshitoshi shows Hideyoshi blowing the conch shell to order the attack.

closest retainer band. Kato Kiyomasa and Fukushima Masanori exemplified Hideyoshi's obsession with haste by abandoning the customary rituals surrounding the taking of enemy heads, and instead ordered their followers to tie the heads to branches of green bamboo like bizarre war standards.

As the first of Sakuma's retreating troops came hurtling down into the valley and the road north to Kita-no-sho, Shibata Katsuie realized that the day was lost. Hoping to save as much of his army as he could he ordered a general retreat, and made it safely back to Kita-no-sho castle with Hideyoshi in hot pursuit. In order to complete the operation Hideyoshi continued north and laid siege to Kita-no-sho. All that Shibata Katsuie had left to defend the place were 3,000 survivors of Shizugatake. It was a hopeless situation, but he had done his duty. Katsuie had served Nobunaga all his life and continued to be loyal to his heir, defying the former farmer's son whom he had once commanded. When the third and second baileys of the castle fell Shibata Katsuie retired to the keep with the members of his family and resolved to go to his death in spectacular samurai fashion. The keep was filled with loose straw, which was set on fire, and Shibata Katsuie committed hara-kiri among the flames.

If the death of Katsuie was the occasion for much rejoicing in the pro-Hideyoshi camp, news of the death of Oda Nobutaka would have inspired even greater rejoicing. We left him besieged in Gifu by his brother Oda Nobuo

The night attack at Shizugatake, 1583

Only a few months have passed since the battle of Yamazaki, but Hideyoshi is once again fighting a battle that has been launched after a forced march. We are on a wooded mountain path leading to the fortress of Shizugatake, high above Lake Biwa, one of a handful of rudimentary frontier castles erected by Hideyoshi to protect Kyoto from the north. Two have already fallen to attacks by Shibata Katsuie's impetuous general Sakuma Morimasa, but because Shizugatake is still holding out Hideyoshi has led a rapid reaction force to catch Morimasa while his men are still sitting in vulnerable rudimentary siege lines high on the wooded hills. Hideyoshi is somewhere down in the valley, while along these paths between the cedar trees, their way illuminated only by burning pine torches and moonlight, his leading samurai fight their way along the ridge towards Shizugatake. Here we see one of the 'Seven Spears of Shizugatake', the famous Kato Kiyomasa, fighting in the combat that was to make him famous. An *ashigaru* under the command of Sakuma Morimasa, distinguished by the red flag on his back with three black *mon*, is knocked to one side by Kiyomasa's advance. Kato Kiyomasa has already been very successful, and has ordered one of his followers to tie the severed heads he has taken to a length of green bamboo so that these traditional proofs of valour will not be mislaid. Another *ashigaru* carries Kiyomasa's personal standard that proclaims his allegiance to the Nichiren sect of Buddhism in the words, 'Hail to the Lotus of the Divine Law'. Kato Kiyomasa is wearing a suit of armour and helmet preserved in the Treasure House of the Hommyoji temple in Kumamoto where he is buried. The striking helmet is one of a number of similar designs favoured by Kiyomasa that consisted of an elongated helmet bowl built up over a simple iron helmet as an extravagant version of an imperial courtier's ceremonial cap. This one has Kiyomasa's *mon* of a gold annulus on either side of it, a design that is replicated on his breastplate. His spear has a crescent moon cross blade.

This woodblock print shows the exact nature of the battle of Shizugatake, which was fought at night along the mountain paths of the range on which were built Hideyoshi's frontier fortresses.

while Hideyoshi fought the battle of Shizugatake. Nobutaka fled from Gifu pursued by Nakagawa Sadanari. Fearing that he was about to be captured, he sought sanctuary in the Shohoji temple in Owari and committed suicide. One more source of opposition to a Hideyoshi takeover had been wiped out.

The successful defeat: Komaki–Nagakute, 1584

At the beginning of the 12th year of Tensho (1584) all the supposed followers of the infant Samboshi of the Oda bloodline were requested by Oda Nobuo to attend new year festivities to offer good wishes to the child. Hideyoshi pointedly did not attend, which infuriated Nobuo, and we do not have to wait long before we hear of Hideyoshi's supposedly former protégé looking around for new allies who would support his cause. Nobuo soon found one in the person of Tokugawa Ieyasu, whose military strength, geographical location and independence of thought and action made him the only daimyo within easy marching distance who could conceivably bring a halt to the seemingly irresistible rise of Toyotomi Hideyoshi.

The subsequent Komaki–Nagakute campaign that followed, named from the castle in Owari that provided the pivot of action and its major battle, was unique in the career of Toyotomi Hideyoshi in that it was a military defeat. Yet so well did Hideyoshi handle the resulting situation that the ultimate outcome proved as successful for his future as any of his great victories, and this was entirely due to Hideyoshi's consummate ability to negotiate a settlement from whatever position he found himself in.

Tokugawa Ieyasu was indeed a formidable opponent. Secure and independent on the Tokaido, in 1582 he had assisted Nobunaga's son Nobutada in the destruction of the Takeda and had been celebrating that achievement with Nobunaga when the fateful request from Hideyoshi for reinforcements against the Mori had arrived. Being unable to take any meaningful part in the subsequent curtailment of Akechi Mitsuhide's ambitions he had waited on the sidelines, busying himself in the administration of the former Takeda provinces of Kai and Shinano, which he had received from Nobunaga as a reward. This also involved absorbing into his army many hundreds of former Takeda retainers, so his military resources were considerable. By 1583, when Hideyoshi was busy with the Shizugatake campaign (which Ieyasu also chose to avoid) he was a daimyo of five provinces, and it was clearly only a matter of time before their spheres of influence collided. At that time the provinces they controlled were divided from one another by Owari, the home of Oda Nobuo, who was to play a major role in matters as they unfolded in 1584.

The story of the Komaki–Nagakute campaign of 1584 has conventionally been told from the Tokugawa point of view, which is only fitting as Ieyasu was the military victor at Nagakute. He also made the first move by entering into a formal alliance with Oda Nobuo, whose possession of Owari province made him the next-door neighbour of Ieyasu in Mikawa. This meant that any campaign Ieyasu undertook could be seen as loyalty to the Oda cause. The 'loyalty to Nobunaga's memory' argument may have been wearing a little thin by 1584, but at least it meant that Ieyasu was not acting overtly for his own selfish reasons. He also safeguarded his eastern border by marrying his daughter to Hojo Ujinao (1562–91), whose mighty family held sway in the fertile Kanto plain ('East of the Barrier') beyond the Hakone Mountains.

Hideyoshi had also been making alliances. The peace agreement he had arranged during the siege of Takamatsu with the Mori had held firm and he had also reached an understanding with Uesugi Kagekatsu (1555–1623) who had the potential to threaten Ieyasu from Echigo province in the north. Yet his first moves towards Ieyasu were peaceful ones, and the offers he made were both genuine and generous. If Ieyasu pledged loyalty to Hideyoshi then he would be given not only Mino province, seat of the late and unlamented Oda Nobutaka, but also Owari, the fief of the very-much-alive Oda Nobuo, who was clearly dispensable. If Ieyasu had agreed it would have meant the end of Nobuo and the Oda cause, but he refused. This may have come as a surprise to Hideyoshi, who had been making overtures to three of Nobuo's senior retainers for them to betray their master and make the transfer easier, but Nobuo had them executed and, whether or not he knew that his province had been offered to Ieyasu, called upon the latter for help against Hideyoshi.

In spite of their personal strengths, neither Hideyoshi nor Ieyasu believed that a defeat of the other was possible unaided, so a confusing array of alliances, orders, plots and counter-plots began at almost every point of the compass from the Hideyoshi/Ieyasu 'frontline states'. These operations involved Maeda Toshiie and Sassa Narimasa to the north of Kyoto, the involvement of warrior monks on the Kii peninsula, and even overtures from Ieyasu to Mori Terumoto to persuade him to break his long-standing agreement. But the most important developments occurred within the territories owned by Oda Nobuo where their borders met. During the second lunar month of Tensho 12 (March 1584) Wakizaka Yasuharu captured Iga-Ueno castle in Iga province on Hideyoshi's behalf. This lost Iga province to Nobuo and was effectively the first move of the Komaki–Nagakute campaign. Hideyoshi left Osaka on 18 April and arrived at Sakamoto near

The most formidable opponent fought by Hideyoshi was Tokugawa Ieyasu, shown here in a painted scroll in Mito. In 1584 Ieyasu defeated Hideyoshi at the battle of Nagakute, although the overall result of the Komaki–Nagakute campaign was in Hideyoshi's favour. The main loser, however, was Oda Nobuo.

Kyoto on 20 April, where he launched his own moves against Nobuo and Ieyasu in two different areas and within days of each other.

The first operational theatre was Ise and western Owari, where Oda Nobuo had moved to secure the castles of the three senior retainers he had executed. On 22 April Kameyama in Ise fell to Nobuo, so Hideyoshi sent Gamo Ujisato, Hasegawa Hidekazu and Takigawa Kazumasu to secure it. They were unable to take it by assault, so laid siege to it and also attacked Nobuo's castle of Mine. That same day, 23 April, Ieyasu moved into Owari to join Nobuo at Kiyosu, from where a relieving force was sent to Kuwana castle. Meanwhile Tsutsui Junkei began to starve out the defenders of Matsugashima, which took three weeks. Mine castle was to fall on 25 April, followed by nearby Kambe on 30 April.

On arriving in Kiyosu to help defend Ise, Ieyasu received news that Hideyoshi had opened a 'second front' using two daimyo who owned castles in Mino. They were Ikeda Tsuneoki (1536–84, also called Nobuteru) of Ogaki castle and his son-in-law Mori Nagayoshi (1558–84, of a different family from the Mori of western Japan), the lord of Kaneyama castle. They had previously received requests for support from Oda Nobuo, who reminded the pair of their long-standing loyalty as *fudai* (hereditary vassals) to the Oda line, of which he was now the true heir. Ikeda Tsuneoki was well aware of this because his son Terumasa (1564–1613) had once been sent as a hostage to serve Oda Nobuo, but while he hesitated over his response a further missive arrived from Hideyoshi offering him the provinces of Mino and Owari, which Ieyasu had so unexpectedly turned down. To be given control over the provinces that were once the fief of his late master Oda Nobunaga was a very tempting offer, particularly when the alternative was to throw in his lot with Nobunaga's dubious second son, so Ikeda consented. It was a decision that was to cost both him and his son-in-law their lives.

On 23 April Ikeda Tsuneoki left Ogaki castle and proceeded eastwards to secure Inuyama, a fortress situated magnificently above the Kisogawa on the border between Mino and Owari. He had once owned Inuyama castle so was familiar with its dramatic topography, and the rule of the Ikeda was also remembered with affection by many within the castle, one of whom arranged for a particular location to be carelessly unguarded, thus allowing a unit of Ikeda samurai to be ferried across the Kiso River unchallenged. Its commander, Nakagawa Sadanari (who had been responsible for the death of Oda Nobutaka in 1583), had recently been killed in a private feud, leaving the defence of the castle in the hands of a valiant Zen monk who fought bravely before he was overcome.

Not wishing to be outdone by his father-in-law in their service to Hideyoshi, Mori Nagayoshi also made a move against Ieyasu's sphere of influence in general and Oda Nobuo's fief in particular. His objective was the castle of Haguro, which lay in Owari to the south of Inuyama on a direct route to Oda Nobuo's headquarters at Kiyosu. On 25 April with 3,000 men under his command he left Kaneyama and bore down upon Haguro, setting up camp for the night at a place called Hachimanbayashi. Unfortunately for him, Ieyasu had already moved up from Kiyosu in response to Ikeda Tsuneoki's operation and had set up his headquarters halfway between Kiyosu and Haguro on the hill of Komakiyama, which at 200m was the only high ground for miles around. Sakai Tadatsugu had been tracking Mori Nagayoshi's movements on Ieyasu's behalf, and requested permission to attack. Ieyasu agreed, so Sakai was joined by Matsudaira Ietada and Okudaira Nobumasa at Komaki, from where they launched a dawn attack on Mori Nagayoshi's headquarters at Hachimanbayashi. Okudaira Nobumasa followed up fierce arquebus fire with a spirited charge and Sakai Tadatsugu led an encircling movement to his rear. Somehow Mori Nagayoshi managed to break through and retreated to Haguro under hot pursuit, leaving the battle of Komaki (or Haguro as it is sometimes called) as a distinct victory for the Tokugawa. Many of Nagayoshi's army did not stop retreating until they reached either Inuyama or Kaneyama, leaving behind on the battlefield the body of one loyal and prominent retainer called Norosuke Za'emon, whose memorial now marks the battle site. Frustrated at his son-in-law's failure, Ikeda Tsuneoki dispatched a further 3,000 troops under Inaba Ittetsu to Haguro, to which Ieyasu responded by moving troops there from Komaki. Ittetsu avoided contact, so Ieyasu also pulled back.

At this point it was suggested to Ieyasu that Komaki should be secured lest a repeat attempt was made. There was already a very dilapidated castle on its summit, so his men rebuilt it along with two other castles nearby. This was Oda Nobuo's territory, not Tokugawa Ieyasu's, but it was Ieyasu who was making all the strategic decisions. These also included the repair of two other old castles at Hira and Kobata, which further protected the approaches to Nobuo's Kiyosu and the border with Ieyasu's own province of Mikawa.

At this point Toyotomi Hideyoshi makes his first personal appearance in the campaign. Fully intending to engage Ieyasu in battle, he proceeded as far as Gifu. From there he continued to Unuma where he crossed the Kisogawa on a pontoon bridge. He then entered Ikeda Tsuneoki's Inuyama castle on 7 May. From Inuyama he took the road south to inspect the condition of his outposts around Haguro, where a series of tiny forts snaked cautiously towards the Tokugawa position on Komakiyama. Gakuden lay at the rear of Hideyoshi's forts and was linked in three places at Uchikuboyama, Sotokuboyama and Komatsuji to three other forts that lay at an angle to them, making a 'front line'. To further strengthen this position, which was dominated by the hostile Komakiyama from a very close distance, Hideyoshi built a rampart to link these three forward forts (Iwasakiyama, Tanaka and Futaebori) over a distance of over 2km. The rampart was 4.1m high and 2m thick, and was pierced by several gates to allow a counter-attack. It was essentially a more substantial version of the loose palisades that had proved so successful at Nagashino. Hideyoshi set up his headquarters at Gakuden and waited for Ieyasu to make a move.

Ieyasu also strengthened his defence line that was anchored at its eastern extremity on Komaki, which does not appear to have been as substantial as Hideyoshi's. It was certainly fortified for part of its length but otherwise consisted of a military road linking six forts in all. From these two defensive complexes Hideyoshi and Ieyasu began to glare at one another, both fearing to make the mistake of a frontal attack and suffer the consequences of Nagashino. After a period of boredom Ikeda Tsuneoki suggested a way by which Ieyasu could be outwitted. If Tsuneoki led a raid into Mikawa province via a wide circling movement to the rear of Komaki and out of sight of it then Ieyasu would be forced to respond and draw troops away from the line. With Ieyasu's defence reduced, Hideyoshi could then mount a direct assault against his weakened army. Hideyoshi gave his consent, but warned Tsuneoki not to be drawn too far into Mikawa or his move would have the opposite effect of weakening Hideyoshi. Ikeda led away 20,000 men at midnight on 15/16 May, arranged in four divisions: Ikeda Tsuneoki (6,000 men), Mori Nagayoshi (3,000 men), Hori Hidemasa (3,000 men) and Miyoshi Hidetsugu (Hideyoshi's nephew, with 8,000), while Hideyoshi made a diversionary attack against Ieyasu's position to cover their departure. Moving in a wide sweep from Gakuden to the east and south, they headed as directly as secrecy would allow

The Komaki–Nagakute campaign saw Hideyoshi pitted against his most formidable rival, the future shogun Tokugawa Ieyasu. The action centred on a raid into Ieyasu's territory away from the protection of the fortified lines that the two rivals had constructed. Hideyoshi's objective was Iwasaki castle, held for Ieyasu by Niwa Ujishige, who is shown here in effigy as a statue in the museum of the reconstructed Iwasaki castle.

for Ieyasu's capital at Okazaki and came first upon the castle of Iwasaki, held for Ieyasu by Niwa Ujishige with a garrison of only 239 men, who withstood their attack for only two hours. So small was the castle and so rapid the victory that only the vanguard of Ikeda Tsuneoki's army had been engaged. The remaining three divisions were still on the road behind him.

By this time Ieyasu had been advised about the situation. The first report informing him that an army sent by Hideyoshi was making its secret way to Mikawa came from two farmers, and at first Ieyasu refused to believe them, thinking it was a ruse to get him to abandon his position, but his scouts soon confirmed the truth of what they had said. Ieyasu had no choice but to move. He took with him 4,500 men as a vanguard under Mizuno Tadashige followed by himself as the main body with 6,300 and Oda Nobuo as a rearguard with 3,000. He left 6,500 men in the lines at Komaki. Moving directly south from Komaki they passed through the Tokugawa possession of Kobata castle and came upon their quarry by early dawn.

Here, the fact that Ikeda Tsuneoki's raiding force had been strung out along the road while he was successfully engaged at Iwasaki was turned to his considerable disadvantage, and Miyoshi Hidetsugu's rearguard were taken completely by surprise as they ate their breakfast at Hakusanbayashi. The third division under Hori Hidemasa soon realized that Ieyasu was on their tail but were unable to provide much assistance to the fourth division. Instead they prudently withdrew to the village of Nagakute where a ridge with a river in front of it promised some measure of security. Hori Hidemasa ordered his men to hold their fire until the enemy were within 20m and promised 100 koku to any arquebus man or archer who brought down a mounted samurai. The excited Tokugawa troops rushed against Hori's lines and received a withering fire that drove them back, to be rallied only by the arrival on the scene of Tokugawa Ieyasu under his great golden fan standard. Ikeda Tsuneoki and Mori Nagayoshi hurried back from Iwasaki to join their comrades. There was a pause while both armies dressed their ranks, and then at 0900hrs the second phase of the battle of Nagakute began with the Tokugawa arquebusiers blazing away at their opponents. This goaded the two sons of Ikeda Tsuneoki, Terumasa and Motosuke, into attacking Ii Naomasa, who held them off with fierce arquebus fire. Ikeda Tsuneoki moved over to aid his sons, but neither Mori Nagayoshi nor Tokugawa Ieyasu had yet made a move. Nagayoshi was waiting for Ieyasu to support his left wing, whereupon he could take him in flank, but Ieyasu was not fooled. He suddenly charged his whole contingent forward in two sections, and the impact alone disordered Mori Nagayoshi's samurai. Mori Nagayoshi rode up and down in front of his lines and waved his war fan frantically. He stood out conspicuously in his white *jinbaori* (surcoat) and one of the Ii *ashigaru* took careful aim and shot him through the head. It was a very public death and acted as a signal for Oda Nobuo to swoop round and fall on Mori's flank. In vain, Ikeda Tsuneoki sent his men forward in support. The whole Mori force gave way, and Ikeda collapsed on his camp stool knowing that all was lost. A young samurai ran up and speared him through, acquiring a prize head. Not long afterwards one of his sons, Ikeda Motosuke was also killed. By 1300hrs the battle was over. Ieyasu sat down and was shown 2,500 heads of the defeated. He was pleased to hear that their own losses had been less than 600.

At the battle of Nagakute Hideyoshi's raiders were ambushed by Tokugawa Ieyasu's army. Here we see arquebus troops in action on the battlefield as depicted on a modern painted screen in the museum on the site of the battlefield.

Meanwhile, back at the two bases, speculation was growing about the outcome of the expedition. When Hideyoshi heard of the early morning encounter he immediately set off with reinforcements, while Honda Tadakatsu made ready to take him in flank. In fact, it never came to a battle, for Hideyoshi's force was so vast as to make him extremely sympathetic to Honda's bravery, and although they could have annihilated the talented Tokugawa captain they did not even threaten him. Honda therefore carried

Another section of the modern painted screen in the museum on the site of the battle of Nagakute shows the death of Hideyoshi's general Mori Nagayoshi. Wearing a white *jinbaori* (surcoat) Nagayoshi tried to rally his troops, and provided a perfect target for one of Ieyasu's muskets.

on to Kobata, where he met Ieyasu in the safety of the castle, and all Hideyoshi achieved was a token attack on the rear of Ieyasu's army as it retreated into Kobata. Soon both armies were safe behind their lines, and the previous stalemate began again. In fact no frontal attack between the two ever took place at Komaki, and the ramparts were eventually allowed to crumble back into the rice fields.

In any account of the triumphs of Tokugawa Ieyasu that is where the Komaki–Nagakute campaign ends, because both armies withdrew from the Komaki area after a stalemate that had lasted for just over three weeks. Ieyasu indeed pulled back to Okazaki and peace, but Hideyoshi actually went on the offensive. Freed from the threat from Ieyasu he proceeded to use his army to attack the possessions of Oda Nobuo in a manner that sees Hideyoshi behaving in his old style. When these operations are combined with the battle of Nagakute it becomes clear that the real loser in the Komaki–Nagakute campaign was Oda Nobuo, because Hideyoshi, although worsted by Ieyasu, targeted Nobuo's castles one by one, uninterrupted by any third-party help for the forsaken Oda heir.

The first place to fall was Kaganoi (in the modern city of Hashima), the strongest castle on the Kisogawa to the north-west of Kiyosu. Here Hideyoshi let loose a fierce bombardment from firearms and small cannon. He then attacked Takegahana (also within modern Hashima), which was in a low-lying place reminiscent of Bitchu-Takamatsu, so the technique that had triumphed there was repeated using a dyke across the Kisogawa until the defenders were forced to climb trees to avoid the flood. This took a month to achieve, after which Hideyoshi captured Oku castle (modern Ichinomiya in Aichi prefecture) and then returned to Osaka. Meanwhile, his generals in the first theatre of operation in Ise had reduced most of Nobuo's castles there. Hideyoshi met with less success on the river delta around Nagashima, where

Takigawa Kazumasu took Kanie castle and attacked Ono, only to have them rescued by Ieyasu. Yet this proved to be the final stimulus for Hideyoshi to reach some form of agreement with Ieyasu, which he did accompanied by a complex arrangement of castle transference, the return of some captured territories, adoption and hostages, so the Komaki–Nagakute campaign came to a peaceful end. Two years later, when Hideyoshi's power was even more firmly established, he married his sister to Tokugawa Ieyasu and sent his mother to him as a hostage. At that point Ieyasu came to Osaka castle and pledged allegiance.

Beyond the boundaries: from Kii to Shikoku, 1585

The year 1584 is also notable in that it marks the point at which Hideyoshi finally threw off any pretence that he was acting in the interests of the Oda family. Following the conclusion of the Komaki–Nagakute campaign Hideyoshi made several grants of land, including two very symbolic donations to Oda Nobuo and Oda Samboshi. By this move, which was not challenged, Hideyoshi indicated a shift in his relationship with the Oda from him being their vassal to them becoming his. A review of the provinces Hideyoshi controlled at the time is also revealing, because through direct rule, control by vassals or prudent alliances Hideyoshi could now exert influence over 37 provinces.

Hideyoshi's conquest of the islands, 1585–87

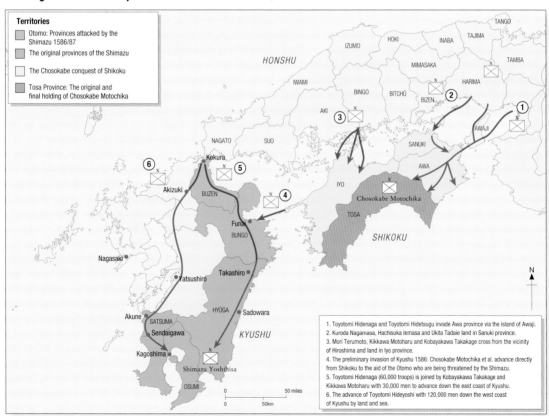

Territories

- Otomo: Provinces attacked by the Shimazu 1586/87
- The original provinces of the Shimazu
- The Chosokabe conquest of Shikoku
- Tosa Province: The original and final holding of Chosokabe Motochika

1. Toyotomi Hidenaga and Toyotomi Hidetsugu invade Awa province via the island of Awaji.
2. Kuroda Nagamasa, Hachisuka Iemasa and Ukita Tadaie land in Sanuki province.
3. Mori Terumoto, Kikkawa Motoharu and Kobayakawa Takakage cross from the vicinity of Hiroshima and land in Iyo province.
4. The preliminary invasion of Kyushu 1586: Chosokabe Motochika et al. advance directly from Shikoku to the aid of the Otomo who are being threatened by the Shimazu.
5. Toyotomi Hidenaga (60,000 troops) is joined by Kobayakawa Takakage and Kikkawa Motoharu with 30,000 men to advance down the east coast of Kyushu.
6. The advance of Toyotomi Hideyoshi with 120,000 men down the west coast of Kyushu by land and sea.

From this position he could contemplate extending his rule well beyond what had been Oda Nobunaga's sphere of influence, and the year 1585 was to find Hideyoshi engaged in three important campaigns beyond these invisible borders, the first of which was against the warrior monks of Negorodera and Saiga. On 9 April an army of 6,000 men under the command of Miyoshi Hidetsugu, Hideyoshi's nephew, and Hashiba Hidenaga, Hideyoshi's half-brother, entered Kii province. They crushed four minor outposts, and on the 23rd day of the same month approached Negorodera from two separate directions. At that time the monks' military strength was believed to be between 30,000 and 50,000 men, and their skills with firearms were considerable. Hideyoshi's army put into operation the crudest (but often most effective) tactic in samurai warfare for use when the enemy are occupying a large complex of wooden buildings. Beginning with the priests' residences, the investing army systematically set fire to the complex and cut down the warrior monks as they escaped from the flames.

Nearby Ota castle, the garrison of which was now considerably increased by fleeing monks at the expense of food supplies, was under the command of Ota Munemasa. The defences of Ota made a fire attack impractical, so in a further application of his favourite flooding technique Hideyoshi ordered the building of a dyke to divert the waters of the Kiigawa and flood the castle. Because of the local topography, building the dam along the north, west and south sides of the castle was a more difficult proposition than at Takamatsu, but a long palisade was begun at a distance of about 300m from the castle walls and packed with earth to make a dam. On the eastern side the dyke was left open to allow the waters in. By 9 May the waters of the Kiigawa were beginning to rise around the castle walls. Heavy rain helped the process along, isolating the garrison more completely from outside help. Nevertheless, the defenders hung on, encouraged at one point by the partial collapse of a section of Hideyoshi's dyke, which caused the deaths of several besiegers as water poured out. Yet soon hunger began to take its toll, and on 21 May the garrison surrendered, led by 50 leading samurai who committed a defiant act of hara-kiri. The remaining soldiers, peasants and women and children who were found in the castle were disarmed of all swords and guns. Those found to be of samurai families were beheaded, while the peasants were sent back to their fields.

Hideyoshi's major campaign of 1585 was his 'D-Day Landing' on Shikoku. In its meticulous organization, complex logistics and coordination Hideyoshi's seaborne invasion recalls his other campaigns in many points of detail. Yet there is one very important difference, because the operations against Shikoku were entirely delegated to others. Absent were the personal involvement and the rapid marching and besieging that had characterized Takamatsu, Yamazaki and Shizugatake. From 1585 onwards Hideyoshi begins to behave more like Oda Nobunaga in the years following Nagashino. He controls the politics of alliance, works out the strategy and then leaves the tactical decisions largely to his trusted allies and vassals, moving on to the scene later to consolidate his victories. This was a model that was to characterize the remainder of

This modern painting in the Noshima Murakami Navy Museum in Miyakubo on the island of Oshima in the Inland Sea depicts the invasion of Shikoku in 1585. Hideyoshi's application of overwhelming force crushed the old-fashioned part-time samurai army of Chosokabe Motochika.

Hideyoshi's military campaigns with the possible exception of Odawara, where little actual fighting was involved.

There is no need to go into the details of how it had taken Chosokabe Motochika (1539–99) 25 years to conquer the whole of Shikoku, except to contrast it with the month it took him to lose it. In fact poor Motochika had only one year in which to enjoy his triumph, because in 1585 he was faced with the considerable resources of Toyotomi Hideyoshi, whose invasion began by using psychological warfare. Rumours created by Hideyoshi's spies of an imminent incursion by a mighty army began to spread around the island. Chosokabe Motochika was so alarmed that he sent a retainer to Osaka to ascertain the truth, and the man returned with an offer. Motochika must surrender all his conquests and pledge allegiance to Hideyoshi. He would then be reinvested with Tosa province.

The furious and proud Motochika refused to settle, so Hideyoshi's invasion force set sail to a background of intimate knowledge about available ports, castle strengths and likely sympathizers to attack the three northerly provinces of Shikoku in a coordinated operation. An army of 30,000 men under the command of Hashiba Hidenaga and 60,000 men under Hashiba Hidetsugu rendezvoused on Awaji Island and sailed to Awa province in 700 vessels. A further army of 23,000 men under Kuroda Nagamasa, Hachizuka Iemasa and Ukita Hideie landed on the island of Yashima, off Sanuki. Farther to the west an army of 60,000 men under Mori Terumoto and his sons Kobayakawa Takakage and Kikkawa Motoharu invaded Iyo.

Chosokabe Motochika set up his headquarters at Hakuchi castle in the centre of the island. He commanded only 8,000 men in total, but it was not through numbers alone that Motochika's men felt overwhelmed, because the psychological warfare continued using the application of 'shock and awe'. The first of Motochika's retainers to be invited to surrender his castle reported to his master that the invading army wore armour 'encased with gold and silver'. Their horses were 'large and fierce-looking' and made the Tosa mounts look like ponies or even dogs. Tosa saddles were made of wood, and their part-time samurai called 'ichiryo gusoku' ('one field and one suit of armour') wore armour that was hanging by threads. Their army was hopelessly outclassed by forces that were virtually professional soldiers. Once his other retainers also began to urge surrender Motochika's initial fury at their attitude turned to grudging acceptance and, just as Hideyoshi had promised, Motochika was spared and allowed to keep only Tosa, while the other three provinces were given to Hideyoshi's retainers. To behave in such a way to a defeated enemy was unprecedented, but there were good reasons for it. Now that he was moving beyond Nobunaga's borders the perils of exerting distant control had become obvious. The Chosokabe were well established in Shikoku, and to leave Motochika in control in return for a pledge of loyalty was a calculated risk to ensure future stability.

The victim of Hideyoshi's third campaign in 1585 was not treated quite so generously. Sassa Narimasa (1539–88) of Etchu had taken Ieyasu's side during the Komaki–Nagakute campaign and in 1585 was cornered in his

The invasion of Shikoku, 1585

An armed beach landing is being carried out on the shores of Shikoku. This was Hideyoshi's 'D-Day' that led to the conquest of this vital area of Japan, and provided the blueprint for the later Kyushu Campaign and the invasion of Korea, whereby tens of thousand of troops were successfully conveyed across water in an application of overwhelming force. In the rear we see numerous samurai disembarking from the ataka-bune type of warships. Their commanders are already ashore, and are amazed that the beach appears to have been abandoned by its defenders. One however is brought before them, held by two samurai grasping his arms and his pigtail. He is a samurai of the Chosokabe family, whose threadbare armour characterizes his status as an ichiryo gusoku, the part-time farmer samurai who had served Chosokabe Motochika so well for many years, but who were to be completely overwhelmed by the professional armies of Toyotomi Hideyoshi. The Chosokabe mon appears on the breastplate of his simple foot-soldier armour. He is nevertheless defiant as he is dragged in front of Toyotomi Hidetsugu, the leader of this sector of the invasion. Toyotomi Hidetsugu was the nephew of Hideyoshi and served his uncle in many campaigns. In 1591 Hideyoshi adopted him as his heir, but later disinherited him when Hideyori was born. He was ordered to commit hara-kiri in 1595 after treason was suspected, but this is many years in the future. Here Hidetsugu leads his uncle's army, dressed splendidly and in complete contrast to the poor Chosokabe samurai. Hidetsugu is shown here in his magnificent red and black armour now owned by the Suntory Museum. It is of nuinobe-do style laced in red sugake odoshi. The helmet is ornamented with a crab's face as the maedate (frontlet) and its claws as wakidate (side badges). The samurai accompanying him have sashimono flags bearing the paulownia mon of his illustrious uncle, while coming up from the beach are two ashigaru bearing Hidetsugu's personal standards. The first, his o uma jirushi (great standard) is a white fukinuki, the streamers commonly used in the 'boys' festival', which billows out behind him like a windsock. It is securely strapped into a sashimono holder on his back, while he holds onto two cords to steady it. The second, his ko uma jirushi (lesser standard) is a golden gohei, a religious symbol associated with Shinto. As it is not so heavy it is carried in a leather pouch at the man's belt.

castle of Toyama by Maeda Toshiie, with a second hostile army heading towards him from the north in the person of Uesugi Kagekatsu. When Narimasa surrendered, Hideyoshi spared his life but moved him to a distant fief in Kyushu and allowed his former holdings to become part of a greater fief for the loyal Maeda Toshiie.

Hideyoshi's crowning mercy: Kyushu, 1587

Beyond the Mori territories and the island of Shikoku lay the great southern island of Kyushu. Sassa Narimasa had been transferred there to a fief in the small portion of it that had not fallen under the control of the Shimazu family of Satsuma by 1586. The Shimazu conquest had been carried out at a very great distance both from Kyoto and Hideyoshi, yet Satsuma was by no means a cultural backwater. In fact two of the most significant developments in recent Japanese history had happened on Shimazu territory. The first was the shipwreck in 1543 on the island of Tanegashima of a group of Portuguese traders, who had with them the first European-style firearms ever seen in Japan. The local daimyo Shimazu Takahisa (1514–71) immediately realized the potential of these new weapons and authorized their production within his territory, a decision that was the beginning of Japan's military revolution. Six years later St Francis Xavier brought Christianity to Japan when he landed in Satsuma, and for a few years Satsuma became Japan's gateway to Europe.

Hideyoshi's progress through Kyushu was facilitated by the submission of several daimyo before his impressive army. In this illustration Akizuki Tanezane is fooled by Hideyoshi's army appearing with false surrender flags. This scene is from *Ehon Toyotomi Kunkoki*.

With firearms to hand, Shimazu Takahisa asserted his authority over neighbouring Osumi and Hyuga provinces in a series of battles. Following Takahisa's death in 1571, the work of developing the family's sphere of influence was carried on by his four sons. The eldest, Yoshihisa (1533–1611) took the Shimazu to their peak of influence. In 1578 the Shimazu responded to an invasion of Hyuga by Otomo Sorin of Bungo province by destroying the Otomo's expeditionary army at the battle of Mimigawa, and in 1584 they marched north from Satsuma and defeated the Ryuzoji at the battle of Okita-Nawate on the Shimabara peninsula. By 1585 they were making plans for the conquest of the Otomo's home province, which would have made them masters of almost the whole of Kyushu. This prospect, however, prompted the intervention of Toyotomi Hideyoshi, who launched the invasion of Kyushu in the name of helping the Otomo. It was the largest military operation ever conducted in Japan up to that time and was Hideyoshi's greatest challenge. The precedents were not encouraging. No army from Honshu (Japan's main island) had ever managed to control Kyushu.

Hideyoshi's conquest began with two advanced operations by Chosokabe Motochika and Sengoku Hidehisa, mounted at the end of 1586. This did little to forestall the advance of the

Shimazu against the Otomo, but they were only the forerunners of a massive expedition involving 250,000 troops raised from 77 daimyo. Toyotomi Hidenaga (the family name had changed from Hashiba to Toyotomi in 1585) led the advance down the eastern coast of Kyushu, while Hideyoshi took the western route. Hidenaga's advance prompted the Shimazu to withdraw from Funai, their farthest gain within the Otomo territory, and to retreat into Hyuga province where they made a stand against him at Takashiro. By the time that the castle fell Hideyoshi was on his way by the other route, meeting with so little opposition that his advance was more like a royal progression. By the end of May Hideyoshi had reached Yatsushiro in Higo province, where the daimyo of the outlying islands and the jagged peninsula around Nagasaki came to join him. The first Shimazu opposition on the west was only encountered at the Sendaigawa, the river that provided a distant outlying moat to the Shimazu capital of Kagoshima. Here a fierce battle took place. Niiro Tadamoto of the Satsuma force led his men in a wild charge against Hideyoshi's lines as they were being re-formed, and could even have broken through to Hideyoshi's headquarters had he not been stopped. In the end sheer weight of numbers overcame the Shimazu, who pulled back to Kagoshima covered by a charge of mounted samurai.

A siege of Tsurumaru castle, the Shimazu headquarters in the middle of modern Kagoshima city, was a daunting prospect. It lay beside a bay, in the middle of which stood the volcano of Sakurajima, whose periodic eruptions had provided natural defences for the area in the form of deep meandering gullies of volcanic deposit. But local Buddhist sympathizers offered to guide Hideyoshi's army through, while his 60,000 troops then held in reserve at Akune would advance by sea round the peninsula and attack from the bay under the bulk of Sakurajima. Toyotomi Hidenaga, whose force had now joined his half-brother, would lead the main advance along the main road, while columns under Kato Kiyomasa, Fukushima Masanori and Kuroda Yoshitaka took the secret gully routes. When the move was eventually carried out a

A siege of Tsurumaru castle (the headquarters of the Shimazu family of Satsuma in modern Kagoshima city) would have been a formidable prospect, as indicated by the natural defences shown in this model of the castle in Kagoshima.

planned ambush by the Shimazu was thwarted. Hidenaga was held along the road, but the other two movements through the gullies and by sea caused great alarm, so the Shimazu withdrew to Tsurumaru castle. Faced with overwhelming force the Shimazu went to the negotiation table. Using the Shikoku experience as a useful precedent Hideyoshi was merciful. Satsuma was too remote from Kyoto to be ruled from there, so the Shimazu surrendered and were reinvested in their own province, subject to the customary safeguards.

The harrying of the north: from Odawara to Kunohe 1590/91

Safe behind the Hakone mountains along the Tokaido, the Hojo of Odawara had felt as secure from Hideyoshi's ambitions as had the Shimazu. Their relationship with their nearest neighbour Tokugawa Ieyasu, cemented by the marriage of Ieyasu's daughter to Hojo Ujinao, had reinforced that view, a hope that was to be shattered when Hideyoshi's advance against them in 1590 was led by Ieyasu. Yet this is not to say that the Hojo were complacent. Since the death of Nobunaga the Hojo had given thought to their long-term defence, and from 1589 onwards their preparations became more acute. In one example, Hojo Ujiteru seized all the nearby temple bells for melting down to make gun barrels. In 1590 the decision was made to make a stand in Odawara castle and abandon nearly all the minor outposts, so the garrisons of nearly all the Hojo satellite castles were stripped to the bare minimum. Most of their troops were packed into Odawara along with the wives and children of the senior retainers so that their courage did not falter.

Hojo Ujiteru's Hachioji castle and Hojo Ujikuni's Hachigata castle came under concerted attack when Hideyoshi advanced. Troops under Uesugi Kagekatsu and Maeda Toshiie spread 35,000 troops round Hachigata, and after a month-long siege Ujikuni surrendered, thus providing a foretaste of what was to come at Odawara. Hachioji, to the west of Edo (modern Tokyo) was also attacked. Hojo Ujiteru, the second son of Hojo Ujiyasu, was not present in Hachioji when Hideyoshi attacked it but was in Odawara, where it was believed that he was most needed. Ujiteru reckoned that Hachioji's topography would enable it to withstand an attack, because the castle was indeed well situated, with the main approach being along a narrow valley, through which rushed a river. A total of 50,000 men attacked Hachioji's garrison of only 1,300. It is often hyperbole to say that the river ran red with the blood of the slain, but in the case of Hachioji it is probably literally true when the corpses fell into the narrow mountain stream. Ghost stories are included in contemporary accounts of the slaughter at Hachioji, with tales of the sounds of hoof-beats and fighting being heard long after the

The Odawara Campaign of 1590, and the achievement of reunification, 1591

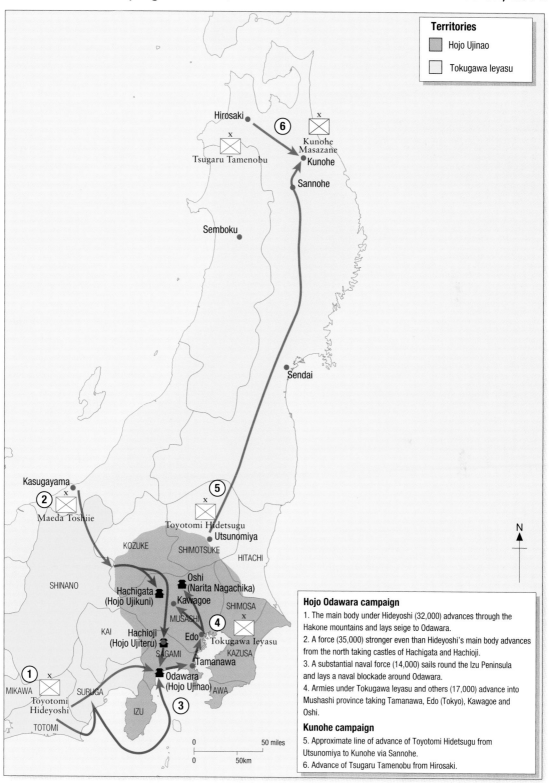

Territories
- Hojo Ujinao
- Tokugawa Ieyasu

Hojo Odawara campaign

1. The main body under Hideyoshi (32,000) advances through the Hakone mountains and lays seige to Odawara.
2. A force (35,000) stronger even than Hideyoshi's main body advances from the north taking castles of Hachigata and Hachioji.
3. A substantial naval force (14,000) sails round the Izu Peninsula and lays a naval blockade around Odawara.
4. Armies under Tokugawa Ieyasu and others (17,000) advance into Mushashi province taking Tamanawa, Edo (Tokyo), Kawagoe and Oshi.

Kunohe campaign

5. Approximate line of advance of Toyotomi Hidetsugu from Utsunomiya to Kunohe via Sannohe.
6. Advance of Tsugaru Tamenobu from Hirosaki.

The 1590 siege of Odawara castle, the seat of the Hojo family, was a fairly peaceful affair, unlike the heavy fighting that took place to control the Hojo's satellite castles. This is the important castle of Hachioji, where the mountain stream literally ran red with blood.

battle had finished. The women of the castle jumped to their deaths from the towers rather than be captured by the Toyotomi forces, and on the anniversary of the battle, 23 June according to legend, the waters of the river turn red once again.

The fall of Hachigata and Hachioji increased the isolation of Odawara, as did one further siege conducted by Ishida Mitsunari against Oshi castle in Musashi province. Oshi, which was commanded by Narita Nagachika, was a castle where the defence depended very much on the stretches of water that surrounded it. Showing that he had learned much in the service of his master Hideyoshi, Ishida Mitsunari converted the defensive waterways into an offensive weapon and flooded Oshi.

Meanwhile, outside Odawara, Hideyoshi was conducting the most theatrical siege in Japanese history. The siege lines became a town in their own right where the besiegers loudly proclaimed their wealth of wine, women and song to the miserable Hojo defenders cooped up inside. They sang, played the board game go, enjoyed theatrical performances and were permitted to have their wives with them. The only significant attack on the castle during the four-month-long siege was conducted by Tokugawa Ieyasu more as a relief from boredom than a meaningful military operation. Miners brought down a section of the walls and an assault was mounted. Yet in spite of the relatively bloodless conduct of the siege itself, when the Hojo finally surrendered they were not treated like the Shimazu. Theirs were not distant provinces where an ancestral hand was needed to control them. Instead the Hojo fief was confiscated and given to Tokugawa Ieyasu, while several compulsory suicides followed among the highest reaches of the family.

Historians with the benefit of hindsight have tended to see the fall of the Hojo as the final move in Hideyoshi's war of reunification, after which the surrender of the vast provinces to the north of Odawara become a footnote to the inevitable triumph. But that was not how Hideyoshi viewed the situation when he returned to Kyoto. His mood was sober, not victorious, because the unconquered lands beyond modern Tokyo represented one third of Japan, where there still remained a handful of strong daimyo who had fought each other for decades as if they were living on another planet. Yet as the months went by the image of Toyotomi Hideyoshi as the magnanimous victor in Kyushu and the ruthless conqueror of the Hojo began to concentrate several minds. Over the past few years Hideyoshi had also enacted the various edicts concerning land ownership, weapon possession and social status (described below), and the northern lords began to realize that they would not be exempt from the new developments. Their collapse began with the meek submission of their strongest member, Date Masamune (1566–1636), who arrived as a supplicant in Hideyoshi's camp while the siege of Odawara was still in progress. His pledge of allegiance and subsequent reinvestment in his own territories achieved peacefully for Date Masamune the same settlement that had ended the Kyushu campaign and avoided any destruction similar to the fate of the Hojo at Odawara. That was the precedent Hideyoshi needed, so from Odawara Hideyoshi proceeded northwards for a final campaign and based himself at Utsunomiya.

Another suspicious northern daimyo was Nambu Nobunao (1546–99) who was located in Sannohe castle in Mutsu province at the northern tip of Honshu. Following Masamune's lead, Nambu Nobunao journeyed to Utsunomiya for an audience with Hideyoshi and there pledged his allegiance. Upon submission he received a document authenticated with Hideyoshi's vermilion seal. It was to be the model for many others that followed, and read:

1. The seven counties in the Nambu area shall be the property of Daizen Daibu [Nobunao].
2. The wife and first son of Nobunao shall remain in Kyoto as hostages.
3. Fiefs shall be surveyed cadastrally and rice collected in the form of a tax in order to support the cost of supporting his wife and child in Kyoto.
4. All the residential castles of the vassals shall be demolished and the wives and first sons of them shall stay in Sannohe.
5. Those who object to the aforementioned shall be punished.

Similar documents accompanied the settlement of all the daimyo who submitted bloodlessly to Hideyoshi after Odawara. It was the lesser daimyo who objected most vociferously, but they were the ones who had fought each other with a casual disregard for political and military developments elsewhere in Japan. Clause four in Nambu Nobunao's document required their castles to be demolished, and one particular instance of objection to this process was to result in the final campaign of Hideyoshi's unification programme. Kunohe Masazane, lord of Kunohe castle in Mutsu, refused to accept the conditions placed upon him by Nambu Nobunao and rose in revolt. As far as he was concerned his insurrection was a rebellion directed against the new powers asserted by Nobunao. But as Nobunao was merely executing the settlement he had received from Hideyoshi it was very easy for him to appeal to Hideyoshi for aid, so Hideyoshi dispatched an army under Toyotomi Hidetsugu against Kunohe castle. It was the furthest north that his troops were ever to march, and with the assistance of Nambu Nobunao the uprising was crushed. There were to be some sporadic incidents of a similar nature in the far north of Japan for a decade to come, but these were essentially diehard

The peaceful submission of the great daimyo of Tohoku (northern Japan) Date Masamune, provided the example to his fellow lords that Hideyoshi needed if he was to complete a bloodless conquest of the remote provinces north of modern Tokyo. This bust of Date Masamune is in Sendai.

On his way to attack Tottori castle Hideyoshi entertains his men with a musical performance on a *sho*, the Japanese 'pan pipes'.

protests against the new regime of resettlement and taxes that Hideyoshi imposed over the next few years through his local representatives. That Japan was now reunified was not open to question, but that this had been carried out by the foot-soldier son of a farmer was cause for amazement.

OPPOSING COMMANDERS

Prior to the Honnoji coup of 1582 Hideyoshi conducted military campaigns on Oda Nobunaga's behalf, and even though Nobunaga was not an opposing commander as such, his example is a good place to begin an assessment of Hideyoshi's comparative greatness, and the most noticeable difference between them is the speed of their achievements. Oda Nobunaga fought the Asai and the Asakura for four years and took ten years to eclipse the power of Takeda Shingen and his son Katsuyori, while none of Hideyoshi's campaigns lasted for more than six months. Through these rapid victories Hideyoshi achieved the reunification of Japan within nine years of Oda Nobunaga's death. For the first two years he carried out a series of military operations in the name of Nobunaga's heir and threw off that pretence only when he began to move beyond Nobunaga's former sphere of influence. In a series of increasingly massive campaigns he carried all before him where the difference between Hideyoshi and his rivals became more acute.

As a subordinate general of Nobunaga, of course, Hideyoshi had operated with the sure knowledge that if he encountered any problems then the full strength of the rest of the Oda army was ready to come to his aid, which must have sustained and encouraged him during a time when he encountered several rival commanders who were both skilled and determined. Kikkawa Tsuneie at Tottori and Shimizu Muneharu at Bitchu-Takamatsu are two good examples, but throughout all these actions, at whatever level of command

Hideyoshi was serving, we notice a particular flair and a gift for generalship that sets him head and shoulders above most of the opposition.

It is only when Hideyoshi begins acting on his own behalf with no back-up that we can begin to assess his level of greatness by direct comparison with his peers. Akechi Mitsuhide is the first to provide such a contrast. In his execution of the Honnoji raid Mitsuhide showed himself the equal of Hideyoshi in daring and rapid consolidation, but he suffered from a lack of overall vision (already suggested by his San'indo campaign) and was then hopelessly outclassed and outmanoeuvred at Yamazaki. A year later, with the campaign and battle of Shizugatake, we see Hideyoshi pitted against someone of his own calibre. Shibata Katsuie had served Oda Nobunaga with a loyalty and skill that was second to none. His behaviour at the siege of Chokoji castle in 1570 had shown his determination and loyalty. Facing death from thirst, he had ordered his men to smash the remaining water jars and then led them in a suicidal charge that in fact carried the day for them. By 1583 Katsuie, Nobunaga's *karo* or senior retainer, was the most serious obstacle to Hideyoshi taking over the Oda hegemony. The campaign that followed, which was as decisive for Japan's future as Yamazaki, was to be presented in the adulatory biographies of Hideyoshi as a personal contest between Hideyoshi and Shibata Katsuie, with the latter caricatured as the former Nobunaga general who lacked the vision to appreciate Hideyoshi's destiny and suffered the consequences. This is the way popular history has also chosen to remember it, but different ways of looking at the course of events are to see Shibata Katsuie as the loyalist and Hideyoshi as the usurper, or both Shibata Katsuie and Hideyoshi either as loyal supporters of the Oda line (albeit for different contenders) or as equally cynical manipulators of puppets.

In the event, it was Shibata Katsuie's disobedient general Sakuma Morimasa who brought about his tragic demise. It was a lesson not lost upon Tokugawa

The monkey-like head and the determined aspect of Toyotomi Hideyoshi are perfectly captured in this excellent waxwork of him at the theme park in Ise known variously as the 'Ise Sengoku Jidai mura' or 'Edo Wonderland Ise'.

Ieyasu in 1584, and throughout Hideyoshi's career Ieyasu provided the strongest opposition he was to encounter. At the battle of Nagakute, Hideyoshi, or rather his raiding party under Ikeda Tsuneoki, was defeated by Ieyasu, but it was through other qualities Hideyoshi possessed that the defeat was not turned into a rout. He cautiously decided not to follow Nagakute with a siege of Kobata and instead wisely returned to his base. From there he went on the offensive against Oda Nobuo, having calculated that Ieyasu would not rush to his support. Hideyoshi then negotiated a peace settlement with Ieyasu, but even after Ieyasu's pledge of allegiance in 1586 Hideyoshi remained suspicious of him. His gift to Ieyasu of the Kanto provinces of the Hojo following their defeat at Odawara finally demonstrated the control Hideyoshi had over him, because Ieyasu left the provinces with which he had been associated since birth. He nevertheless treated the whole process in a very positive manner, choosing Edo, now the great city of Tokyo, for his

This hanging scroll of Hideyoshi appears in the Hosei Niko Exhibition Hall, a museum devoted to the memory of Hideyoshi and his contemporary Kato Kiyomasa in Nakamura, Nagoya.

capital rather than Odawara, but the element of control present in an apparent reward for good behaviour is very evident. The move shifted the Tokugawa responsibilities farther to the east, thus allowing more scope for Hideyoshi to consolidate his position.

Throughout his career Hideyoshi knew how to fight battles better than almost everyone he encountered, but his superiority over them was shown even more by the battles he never had to fight. Shikoku was not a war of attrition; Tsurumaru castle in Kagoshima was never besieged and the lands of the minor lords of Dewa Province were never invaded. There is a saying, attributed to Tokugawa Ieyasu, that a sword is in its position of greatest power while resting in its scabbard. Perhaps in that phrase lies the key to understanding Hideyoshi's superiority over his contemporaries.

INSIDE THE MIND

Toyotomi Hideyoshi combined the true general's assets of broad strategy and acute tactical thinking, and skills and patience in siegecraft together with the guile of a subtle politician. He also understood that he could achieve nothing alone, and from the time of his first appointment as a junior officer in Nobunaga's army Hideyoshi was to be supported by a core of followers whose numbers and loyalty grew exponentially as the years went by. Their devoted service, which took them to Korea and back and then led to many of them dying on the field of Sekigahara as they stood firm for Hideyoshi's heir, had much to do with the fact that Hideyoshi had always been a soldiers' general who never lacked the common touch. His rise from the ranks was undoubtedly one of the reasons why he inspired such loyalty and confidence in his followers. Most of his generals were men like him. Several of them had even served in the armies of daimyo defeated by Hideyoshi and had then rushed to pledge service to this brilliant general who had allowed them to retain their heads. Yet the bottom line was always the achievement of victory, and even in the Komaki–Nagakute campaign where Hideyoshi lost a battle he won the war.

Here lies one further aspect of the brilliance of Hideyoshi as a general, and it lies in the talent for diplomacy that made manageable the campaigns that he could not avoid fighting. Accommodation with daimyo like Mori Terumoto and Date Masamune not only made potentially huge endeavours unnecessary, it also provided the future manpower for ventures like Shikoku, where force would always be needed. Oda Nobunaga had destroyed his enemies and rewarded his followers. Hideyoshi of course rewarded his followers, but was very selective about whom he destroyed, and of the 16 richest and most powerful daimyo in Japan at the time of Hideyoshi's death in 1598 only two had been his followers prior to 1582. Nine, in fact, had once been his enemies. Hideyoshi had a mailed fist and a velvet glove, and unlike Nobunaga, he had a perfect grasp of when to be ruthless with those he had conquered and when to be generous.

In his private life this ruthless leader of armies composed numerous tender and affectionate letters to friends and relatives. In this personal correspondence there is always great concern expressed for the recipient's health, just as Hideyoshi himself was also obsessively concerned with his own well-being. As for Hideyoshi's appearance, contemporary observers note his small, wizened stature and his total lack of aristocratic features on a monkey-like head, yet as his power grew Hideyoshi took on aristocratic trappings on a grander scale than any ruler before him except Nobunaga. Nobunaga's palace, the multi-storeyed Azuchi castle, together with Hideyoshi's castle of Fushimi at Momoyama together provide the name for the Azuchi–Momoyama Period, a time of wealth and lavish artistic beauty presided over by the 'Bountiful Minister' – the literal translation of Hideyoshi's final surname of Toyotomi. Hideyoshi's enthusiastic biographer Ota Gyuichi was to write:

> Ever since the advent of the Taiko Hideyoshi, gold and silver have gushed forth from the mountains and from the plains in the land of Japan… In the old days, no one as much as laid an eye on gold. But in this age … our Empire enjoys peace and prosperity; on the roads not one beggar or outcast is to be seen, all on account of the Taiko Hideyoshi's devotion to acts of compassion and mercy.

The lavish decoration of his castles, gardens and palaces, the use of gold leaf for sliding screens and the ostentation of his costume spoke of a Renaissance prince, and above all there was Hideyoshi's passion for the tea ceremony. In his hands this exquisite practice that encapsulated all that was subtle and unworldly in Japanese culture became a tool both of self-expression and of political diplomacy. Through tea ceremonies Hideyoshi communed with nature and with his rivals, but he was not beyond manipulating the tea ceremony for his own ends, as shown by his famous tea ceremony performed for the emperor in a gold-plated tea house.

Hideyoshi's attitude towards organized religion was a pragmatic one, similar to his master Oda Nobunaga. The story is told of Hideyoshi visiting the holy mountain of Koyasan and walking boldly across a certain bridge that promised doom to anyone who was lacking virtue.

Hideyoshi was always a 'soldiers' general', hence the great affection in which he was held and the loyalty he inspired. Here, we see his samurai celebrating, although the party was designed to fool the occupants of the castle he was currently besieging. This scene is from *Ehon Toyotomi Kunkoki*.

Perhaps the most loyal of all Hideyoshi's generals was Ishida Mitsunari, who was defeated at the head of the coalition army that opposed Tokugawa Ieyasu at the battle of Sekigahara in 1600. Mitsunari was a skilled general, and captured the castle of Oshi in 1590 by flooding it after the style of Hideyoshi, but he first came to Hideyoshi's notice because of his expertise at the tea ceremony, a moment captured by this statue in Nagahama.

Thus apparently did Hideyoshi show his contempt for religious belief (although he had allegedly tested out the bridge and its curse in private the night before).

Perhaps the most interesting aspects of Hideyoshi's psychology concerned his predilection for names and titles. The surname Hashiba had sufficed from the time of his acquisition of Omi province, but in 1585 he took the surname by which he is best known: Toyotomi, or 'Bountiful Minister', arguing that because of his origins, admittedly obscure but clearly the result of destiny and miracles, he was obliged to found a new and glorious dynasty. In that same year he received the title of *kampaku* (imperial regent), the highest position in the imperial court system save that of the emperor himself. No one before had ever taken that title unless he belonged to the prestigious Fujiwara family, a problem Hideyoshi solved by having himself adopted by Konoe Sakihisa of the branch of the Fujiwara that had monopolized the office. When the reigning emperor abdicated, Hideyoshi had his own choice of successor: the 16-year-old Go-Yozei. Hideyoshi now dominated the imperial court as *kampaku* and also as Daijo Daijin – grand minister of state. When he passed the title of *kampaku* on to Hidetsugu in 1592 Hideyoshi became known as the Taiko, which also means 'regent'.

Hideyoshi's rise to such dizzy heights may also explain why he did not seize or even manipulate the position that seems so obvious: that of becoming shogun. Nobunaga may have abolished the shogunate in 1573, but Ashikaga Yoshiaki was still around until 1597 and could easily have been forced to adopt Hideyoshi if the latter had desired such a promotion. But speculation about the mystic power of the shogunate is coloured by the fact that Tokugawa Ieyasu was later to revive the shogunate and make it last for two and a half centuries. In 1585 the shogunate did not have such an allure, particularly when Hideyoshi was granted the means of surpassing that moribund institution completely.

WHEN WAR IS DONE

Hideyoshi's domestic policies are inseparable from his military activities. Both had the joint aims of bringing peace to the realm and ensuring that peace was maintained. Although his policies clearly drew on the foundations laid by Oda Nobunaga, Hideyoshi's cadastral surveys, the separation edict, the Sword Hunt and the removal of samurai from the land into an exclusive military environment, were innovative, far-reaching and so successful that the Tokugawa family who took over his empire left them pretty well as they had been for the next two and a half centuries.

Hideyoshi's policy of accommodation with defeated enemies such as the Chosokabe and the Shimazu facilitated the process of his land surveys, a long programme of consolidation that was among the most important of his domestic reforms. The Taiko Kenchi was a process whereby land use and ownership for the whole of Japan was surveyed, valued, reallocated if necessary and placed under the appropriate control so that it could be converted to a tax yield. It was an enterprise that Hideyoshi applied to the nation as a whole in a way that the best daimyo had once tried to do within their own provinces. As a newly created daimyo Hideyoshi had carried out his own land survey in Omi province when he received it in fief after the defeat of the Asai. This process was part of a much larger effort to register all the

A portrait of Toyotomi Hideyoshi as *kampaku* (imperial regent). He is dressed in formal robes. This is a copy of the original painting (dated 1598) that is to be found in the collection of the Kodaiji, Kyoto.

land within the Oda domain, whereby Hideyoshi defined the boundaries of his fief, sorted out any competing claims from warriors who lived there and reviewed the landholdings of religious institutions. Where Hideyoshi's later *kenchi* (land survey) differed from earlier (pre-1580) practices was that it no longer relied solely on possibly misleading reports filed by biased local officials with vested interests. Instead, using the resources now available to him, Hideyoshi sent in official agents for the direct inspection of land, which was assessed thoroughly using a standardized measuring system.

By 1598, the year of Hideyoshi's death, almost all of Japan had been surveyed, but there had also been fierce resistance in several places where the process had provoked riots and uprisings. It was partly for this reason that much of Tohoku remained unsurveyed. There, the Onodera family of Dewa province, for example, fought Hideyoshi's representative Otani Yoshitsugu (otherwise Yoshitaka, 1559–1600) with a vigour reminiscent of the time of civil war, and in Semboku county in Dewa Hideyoshi's *kenchi-bugyo* (land survey magistrates) were to find themselves trapped by rebellious peasants intending to kill them. Yoshitsugu led an army against them and massacres followed together with a confiscation of weapons.

In less remote provinces such rebellions had been successfully pre-empted by the supposedly nationwide Sword Hunt of 1588. Based on a similar programme conducted on Nobunaga's behalf in Echizen in 1575, all weapons of war were seized by Hideyoshi's agents. Small landowners, village samurai and independent-minded temples had removed from them the physical means to challenge the rule of Hideyoshi. A similar edict aimed at seafarers began to control the problem of piracy. But as well as disarming the country a further means of social control was to follow in the form of the Separation Edict of 1591, which stated:

If there should be living among you any men formerly in military service who have taken up the life of a peasant since the seventh month of last year, with the end of the campaign in the Mutsu region, you are hereby authorized to take them under surveillance and expel them... If any peasant abandons his fields ... not only should he be punished but the entire village should be brought to justice with him. Anyone who is not employed either in military service or in cultivating land shall likewise be investigated by the local authorities and expelled.

The image of Hideyoshi as the all-conquering general is perfectly illustrated here as his glare alone thoroughly intimidates Sakuma Morimasa, whom he defeated at the battle of Shizugatake in 1583. This scene is from *Ehon Toyotomi Kunkoki*, an illustrated life of Hideyoshi with woodblock illustrations by Kuniyoshi.

This statue of Hideyoshi depicts him as an ancient court archer.

The Separation Edict therefore defined the distinction between samurai and farmer that was to continue throughout the Tokugawa Period. It also allowed the potential for a reign of terror to be inflicted upon any local population who did not comply with Hideyoshi's wishes, a situation that was to apply almost immediately with the forced recruitment of peasants and fishermen for the forthcoming Korean campaign. Yet the Separation Edict had changed the nature of such recruitment for ever. No longer could a farmer's son like Hideyoshi enlist as a foot soldier and rise to be a general. From now on a peasant who was forced (or even volunteered) to do his duty would not carry out that function with a sword or gun in his hand, but with a cripplingly heavy pack on his back. To the leader of a modern army such as Hideyoshi such a restriction on military manpower was a matter of no concern. He had troops in easy sufficiency and, because of the increased sophistication associated with weaponry, an untrained and undrilled peasant handed an arquebus or a long shafted spear would be a liability rather than an asset.

By the time of Hideyoshi's death in 1598 he was already a legendary figure, and his memory inspired a loyalty to his name and to his family that was to be sustained even by the generals whom he had sent to Korea. The mood of national reverence was expressed at the highest level by the imperial court's decision to build a shrine to him in Kyoto. The Hokoku shrine, or 'shrine of the wealth of the nation' became the centre of the memorialization of the man who by his generalship and leadership had unified Japan. Had circumstances been different the Hokoku shrine would certainly have become recognized as one of the great Shinto shrines of Japan. Instead it survives today as a modest and architecturally undistinguished place within the grounds of the Hokoji temple, which is rarely visited by tourists. Hideyoshi's dynasty did not last long enough for anything else.

When the expeditionary forces who had fought against Korea in the 1590s arrived back in Japan they found a country transformed. Gone was the great general whom they had served so loyally for so long. In his place was Toyotomi Hideyori (1593–1615), his son of five years of age, who was already being manipulated by a council of regents. In October 1600 these seething rivalries erupted in the battle of Sekigahara, where Tokugawa Ieyasu, who alone had worsted Toyotomi Hideyoshi in battle, defeated a coalition of daimyo who stayed loyal to Hideyoshi's heir. By means of the battle of Sekigahara, Tokugawa Ieyasu took over the inheritance of Toyotomi Hideyoshi and became shogun in 1603. Yet it took a further campaign, the great siege of Osaka castle from 1614 to 1615 for Tokugawa Ieyasu finally to overcome Toyotomi Hideyori. Following the destruction of Osaka, and Hideyori with it, Ieyasu closed down the Hokoku shrine, hoping thereby to extinguish reverence for the great commander he had once served.

A LIFE IN WORDS

The two most important early biographies of Toyotomi Hideyoshi are *Taiko-ki* by Oze Hoan (1564–1640) and *Taiko gunki* by Ota Gyuichi (1527–1610), who also wrote a life of Nobunaga. Both are highly complementary and contain much legendary material. *Taiko-ki* also became the first printed biography when it was published in 22 volumes in 1626. By 1626, of course, the Tokugawa shogunate was firmly established, so any literary references to the man whom the Tokugawa had eclipsed had to be very sensitively framed. *Taiko-ki*, therefore, kept scrupulously to the story of the great commander and carefully avoided any discussion of what happened to his son and heir. At the end of the 18th century, *Taiko-ki* reappeared in an illustrated version as *Ehon Taikoki* with a simplified text by Takeuchi Kakusai and lively illustrations by the accomplished artist Okada Gyokuzan. The project was completed between 1797 and 1802, resulting in a series of 84 woodblock-printed books. It proved very popular, and a staged version even entered the repertoire of the kabuki theatre.

Up to this point the authorities seem to have held back from criticism or censorship of this literary treatment of Hideyoshi. *Ehon Taikoki*, it would appear, was no threat to the reputation of the Tokugawa state, but matters were to change when certain famous artists used the *Ehon Taikoki* as material for single-sheet woodblock prints. With their bright colours, dramatic perspective and wide circulation the shogunate sensed danger from these pictures 'of the floating world' (*ukiyo-e*) that were published in their thousands alongside images of actors and sumo wrestlers. So in 1804 an edict was issued forbidding 'single sheet images, books, etc., materials and pictures showing

This modern reproduction of Hideyoshi's famous sunburst helmet, the original of which is now lost, is on display in Osaka castle.

A woodblock print showing Hideyoshi in classic form at the head of a large army and conducting a successful siege of an enemy position.

the names of warriors after the Tensho era [i.e. post-1592] and of course their crests, seals, names, etc.'. Why? Because, according to a separate legal document, such materials 'stimulated criticism of the Tokugawa ancestors'. One of the offending artists, the famous Utamaro, was imprisoned for 50 days.

Half a century later the famous artist Kuniyoshi brought out his own illustrated version of Hideyoshi's biography. Entitled *Ehon Toyotomi Kunkoki*, it consists of 90 volumes. Printing started in 1855 and was completed in 1881, long after Kuniyoshi's death and also after the passing of the Tokugawa. With the Tokugawa shogunate consigned to history, a reassessment could begin of the military reputation of the great commander Toyotomi Hideyoshi.

GLOSSARY

The authentic form of Hideyoshi's golden gourd battle standard would appear to consist of one gourd, as shown here in the reproduction of it on show in Osaka castle.

Ashigaru	Foot soldier.
Ataka-bune	Warship.
Bakufu	The shogunate – 'government within the curtain'.
Daijo Daijin	Great minister of state.
Daimyo	Feudal lord.
Fudai	Inner lords, hereditary retainers.
Gundan	War band – the vassals from whom a daimyo's army would be formed.
Kanpaku	Imperial regent.
Karo	An elder, or senior vassal who would act in the daimyo's absence.
Kerai	A retainer of a daimyo.
Kosho	Pages or squires.
Ko uma jirushi	Lesser standard.
Maku	The curtains that enclosed a general's field headquarters.
Mon	Family badge.
O uma jirushi	Great standard.
Samurai	Japanese knight.
Shogun	The military dictator of Japan.
Sugake odoshi	Spaced-out lacing of armour.
Taiko	Retired regent – a title used by Hideyoshi after 1592.
Tozama	Outer lords who submitted to a daimyo only after being defeated by him or after witnessing his triumph.

FURTHER READING

The edition of *Taiko-ki* I have used in this work was edited by Yoshida Yutaka and published in Tokyo in 1979. There is only one biography of Hideyoshi in the English language. This is the excellent *Hideyoshi* by Mary Elizabeth Berry (Harvard East Asian Monographs: Harvard, 1982). In that book Hideyoshi's life is examined from every angle, showing him as a great statesman in addition to being a great general. *The Life of Toyotomi Hideyoshi* by Walter and M. E. Dening (Kessinger Publishing: Whitefish, MT, 2006) is a historical curiosity published in 1930 and now available as a paperback facsimile from Kessinger Publishing Rare Reprints. Dening drew largely from the fictionalized biographies of Hideyoshi. Hideyoshi's correspondence is used to paint a vivid and accurate picture of the man in *101 letters of Hideyoshi,* translated and edited by Adriana Boscaro (Sophia University: Tokyo, 1975). Excellent discussions of Hideyoshi also appear in *Warlords, Artists, and Commoners: Japan in the Sixteenth Century*, edited by George Elison and Bardwell L. Smith (University of Hawaii Press: Honolulu, 1981). Of particular interest are the essays by George Elison entitled 'The Cross and the Sword: Patterns of Momoyama History' and 'Hideyoshi, the Bountiful Minister'. Several chapters in *The Cambridge History of Japan: Volume Four, Early Modern Japan* (Cambridge University Press: Cambridge, 1991) discuss matters relating to Hideyoshi, and there is a very good discussion of Hideyoshi's far-reaching domestic policies in *Japan Before Tokugawa: Political Consolidation and Economic Growth 1500–1650* edited by John Whitney Hall, Nagahara Keiji and Kozo Yamamura (Princeton University Press: Princeton, 1981). Illustrations from Kuniyoshi's *Ehon Toyotomi Kunkoki* were published in 1975 by W. M. Hawley as *The Pictorial Biography of Toyotomi Hideyoshi, The Unifier of Japan* (Hawley Publications: Hollywood, 1975).

Suit of armour owned by Toyotomi Hideyoshi. The body and skirts of the armour are finished in closely-spaced dark-blue silk lacing with an attractive design of a red rising sun picked out on the breast. There is an extensive use of *mon* (badges) as decoration on the smooth, lacquered, metal surfaces.

This shrine marks Hideyoshi's birthplace in the village of Nakamura, which now lies within the modern city of Nagoya. A photograph of a portrait of the 'Napoleon of Japan', shown in later life in the robes of the *kampaku*, hangs beside the entrance.

INDEX

Note: All names are given in Japanese order with family name first. Figures in **bold** refer to ilustrations